MW01032570

NO CONDITION IS PERMANENT!

*10 Master Strategies To Help You Move
From Fear And Doubt To Action!*

Rene Godefroy

Foreword by Jeffrey Gitomer

An Imprint of InQuest Publishing

No Condition Is Permanent!
by Rene Godefroy

Copyright © 2002, Rene Godefroy

Layout by Irene Archer
Cover designed by John Park and Irene Archer

For more information contact InQuest Publishing,
P.O. Box 725169, Atlanta, Georgia 31139
Toll free: 1-866-275-7363, Atlanta (770) 438-1373.

First Edition, 2002
Printed in the United States of America
Printed on acid-free paper

Library of Congress Cataloging-
in-Publication Data has been applied for.

ISBN: 0-9719754-0-X

Dedication

This book is dedicated to my mother,
Yvette Godefroy, and to Tante Da.

Maman, I take my hat off to you for your relentless
courage in facing life's adversities, and for your untiring
hard work in providing for Andrele, Roberto and me.

Tante Da, thank you for holding my hand
and giving me encouragement.

Contents

Acknowledgements .... *vii*

Foreword by Jeffrey Gitomer .... *xi*

Introduction .... *xv*

CHAPTER 1
Focus On The Finish, Not The Starting Line 1

CHAPTER 2
Believe In Spite Of The Doubters Around You! 19

CHAPTER 3
Learn To Love The Process; It's Precious 35

CHAPTER 4
Stop The Excuses, Please 49

CHAPTER 5
Look for The Stars In Your Darkest Moment 61

CHAPTER 6
See With Fresh Eyes 79

CHAPTER 7
Be Committed, Not Just Interested! 95

CHAPTER 8
Keep Your Attitude Positively Charged..............................113

CHAPTER 9
Create A Positive Reputation...131

CHAPTER 10
Practice Unbounded Gratitude...147

Epilogue *161*
My Favorite Books..*163*

Acknowledgements

In the south, they say that if you see a turtle on the side of the fence, chances are it did not get there by itself. Well, I am one big turtle on the fence of life. This is the hardest part of the whole project for me. It is virtually impossible for me to mention all the people who have directly or indirectly provided me with some kind of assistance—though I have tried. Invariably, I am bound to leave out a few names. Please charge it to my head, not my heart.

First, a special thanks to my editor, Patricia Toles, for your patience and dedication. Pat, you are one of the most insightful people I have ever met. You are truly an editor extraordinaire!

Thanks also to the following people:

Tim Polk for overseeing the project.

Ms. Myrtice V. Bell, my grammarian, for your much-needed assistance.

Myra McElhaney, my mentor, coach and friend. Myra, I am so grateful to you for being there any time I have needed your advice.

Mark Mayberry. Mark, mega thanks to you for showing my video to the selection committee of the National Speakers Association.

Marie Joe Maurice for your support and encouragement through the rough times.

Phil and Bonnie Parker for your love, support, and encouragement.

My cheerleaders: Carol Montrond, Marcia Russell-Cintron, Jerry Lee, Mary Jo Ferrazza, Connie Payton, Jewel Daniels Radford, and Janet Toles. Jan, if it weren't for you I would not have found my editor or grammarian. Thanks for believing in me and for your much needed support.

The giants of the speaking industry who pour so much into my life: Keith Harrell, W. Mitchell, Jeffrey Gitomer, Dave Gordon, Nido Qubein, Dan Burrus, Bill Karlson, Mr. Per, Tracy Brown, Rosita Perez, and Larry Winget.

My friends at the National Speakers Association of Georgia: Shirley Garrett, Doug Smart, Austin McGonigle, Dick Biggs, John Cooper, Marcia Steele, and Valerie Jones. Each of you took time out of your busy schedules to share with me.

My best buddy and brother-in-law, Wes Lafortune. Man, you were the first person to see my dream.

My sister, Andrele Lafortune. Andrele, you gave me my first lesson on how to cross a busy city street. Today, I am still using that lesson as a metaphor for crossing the challenging streets of life.

My brother, Roberto Glemaud. I admire your courage and endurance.

My nieces and nephews: Thomasina, Kelly, Mikelange, Robintina and Jeremy.

Ketty and Jean Calixte. I can still see the day you guys came to pick me up after the truck driver dropped me off somewhere in Brooklyn.

Acknowledgements

Renel Glemaud for not treating me any different when you used to come by to visit my sister and brother.

The rest of my family, especially Barbara Alexandre, Joanne Valme, and Sandra Fenelon. Guys, you are too numerous to mention, but you know who you are.

Angela Schelp. Your bureau was the first to book me after my debut at the National Speakers Association.

The Bell Stand staff at the Waverly Renaissance Hotel. Many of you have supported and believed in me.

All the folks at Speak, Inc. especially, Jeff Bigelow, for keeping me busy.

Finally, thanks to everyone who has ever booked me to speak at a meeting. Many of you discovered me when I was still unknown. You made it all possible for me.

Foreword

∞

HE'S NOT A VILLAGE HERO.
HE'S AN EXAMPLE TO FOLLOW.

"**W**elcome to the Renaissance Waverly Hotel. Can I help you with your bags?" Those are the first words spoken to me by Rene Godefroy.

As he put my bags onto the luggage cart he noticed my book, The Sales Bible.

"Did you write that book?"

"Yes I did." I smiled puffing out my chest a bit.

"How can I get a copy?" he asked without hesitating.

"I'll tell you what, you can get one tonight. Would you rather have a book or a tip?"

"I'll take the book!" he responded with a big smile.

"Are you a member of the National Speakers Association?" Rene asked.

"Yes, I am. How do you know about that organization?" I was a bit taken aback by his question. How does a bellman know about the NSA?

"I'm a member of the Georgia Speakers Association myself, and I plan to join the National this year."

"Cool. Are you a speaker?"

"Yes, I am," he said with the self-assurance of a twenty-year veteran.

We then played the "name-game" for a few minutes. Do you know this guy, do you know that guy. Turns out he knew all the people that mattered, at least all the ones I knew.

"What are you doing working as a bellman?" I wanted to know.

"I'm not making a full-time living as a speaker, so I do this for extra money," he said as he smiled.

This guy sure smiles a lot, I thought.

I wondered how many other speakers in the vaunted National Speakers Association began their careers as bellmen. I think the answer is somewhere between "not many" and "none". Anyway, this guy was kind of cool. He had a sort of a foreign accent.

"Where are you from?"

"Haiti."

"How'd you get to America?"

"Long story," he said. "I'll tell you sometime."

As it turns out, I gave him the book AND a tip. I also invited him to e-mail me if he needed any help in growing his speaking business. I often make that offer to new speakers, but usually no one takes me up on it. The next morning, I got an e-mail from Rene asking my advice about Speaker's Bureaus and bookings. That told me that he was serious and *on top* of his ambition. I love helping people who "want it."

Two months later, I was at the National Speakers Association winter workshop in Norfolk at some big Marriott; and there was Rene. He was wearing a suit, and he looked as dapper and as professional as he possibly could. We were happy to see one another.

"Did you give the bellman a big tip?" I asked. Rene smiled.

I'm always happy when I see someone trying to "make it" and the first thing they do is become a student. We became better friends that weekend. Then the national convention came to Washington, DC. There was Rene. He seemed more excited this time.

"What's going on?" I asked.

"I'm telling my story."

"When's that going to happen?"

"Monday morning on the main platform. They only gave me 30 minutes."

"That's incredible. Do you need any help?"

Rene just smiled and said, "Just pray that I don't mess it up!"

"I think you'll be fine," I said. "I think you'll be just fine."

I got to hear the Rene Godefroy story: how he came to America overcoming every obstacle in his path using sheer determination, risking everything (including his life), and having an attitude of never quit. I was, to say the least, touched by his message and inspired by his unwavering desire to achieve the American dream.

He crushed the audience. Standing ovation.

As you read this book, please understand that there's more to it than Rene's story. Between the lines are the lessons that seem to elude us as adults. As Americans, even after 911, we tend to take everything we have for granted. Rene takes nothing for granted, and is willing to drag other people's bags in the evening while he builds his business during the day so that he can make his mark in the land of the free and the home of the brave.

To the people in his home village, Rene is a hero. He broke away, he came to America, and he is succeeding. Does he send money home to his family? What do you think? He probably sends home too much.

But don't look at Rene simply as a village hero. Look at Rene as a lifelong lesson of persistence and determination, of attitude and work ethic, of self-belief and personal dedication to excellence.

Yes, over the last few years I have inspired Rene, helped him build his business, and encouraged him to succeed; but don't you think for one moment that this young man has not inspired me and thousands of others who have had the privilege of listening to his eloquently told story. It is my hope that after you have finished reading this book you will become a hero in your village, and you will go out and buy several more copies to give to your friends so that they may catch the inspiration of Rene Godefroy.

Jeffrey Gitomer

Introduction

I am delighted you chose to pick up *No Condition is Permanent!* I really mean it. There are so many books you could have bought and read. There is, also, so much that you could have done with your time. Yet, you have chosen to spend your time with me. What's more, you have spent your hard-earned money hoping to find something meaningful to better your life.

First, I want to tell you that you may not agree with everything I have to say. That's good. In fact, one percent of you will find this book offensive. The rest of you will devour every word. Bill Cosby reminds us that the secret to success is found by not trying to please everybody. Winners know that it is virtually impossible to meet everyone's needs. Thus, I have chosen to focus on the 99% of you who will be pleased.

Second, I want to say up front that I don't have all the answers. In fact, I am still seeking just like you are. For many of you, my role is not to teach you anything new. It is to remind you of what you already know. For others of you, some of the things I talk about will sound too basic. Success, whatever that means to you, is not usually something deep and complicated. It is most often found in the mastery of the basics.

I read that when Vince Lombardi took over the losing Green Bay Packers, a reporter asked him what plans he had to turn the team around. Mr. Lombardi replied that he was not going to turn the team around. He said that he was going to get brilliant on the basics. "...*Brilliant on the basics*." Do you get it? Remember this:

your accomplishments in life will not be determined by how much you know. They will be determined by how much you do with what you know. Action is the hinge upon which notable achievement revolves.

Rene Godefroy

CHAPTER ONE

Focus On The Finish Line, Not The Starting Line

Focus On The Finish Line, Not The Starting Line

"Twenty years from now, you will be more disappointed by the things you didn't do than the ones you did. So throw off the bowlines. Sail away from the safe harbor. Catch the trade winds in your sails. Explore. Dream. Discover."—Mark Twain

Many people believe one of the myths of success: that in order to achieve anything significant in life one must come from a background full of resources. There are those who look at where they are in life and conclude that it's impossible to make it to the top. Have you met people like this, those who blame their failure on their past? Somewhere in their subconscious they believe their past (where they started in life) is the reason they are barely surviving today. This is far from the truth. When I look at how far I have come to be where I am today, I can't help thinking that you and I have more inside us than we could ever imagine.

Against All Odds

I was born in extreme poverty in a tiny village in Haiti. Haiti is located south of Florida, with the Atlantic Ocean to the north and the Caribbean Sea to the south. While not all people on the island are poor, the people in my village certainly were. The village is about two miles long and one mile wide. It is located on the extreme southside in the backwoods of Haiti. We had no running water, no plumbing, and no electricity. We didn't have access to medical care. I still remember the first time I saw lights. They were the headlights of an old and battered truck they called Voici Phane (vwah-see fahn), which means here is Phane...the truck owner's name.

Things were difficult in my village. By the time I was five or six years old, I was walking long distances on narrow and danger-ous pathways to collect drinking water from a wellspring, and to fetch wood for cooking. I started climbing coconut and mango trees for survival. As a little boy, I remember using my hands to eat because we had no silverware. For plates, we used half cal-abashes, which are like big watermelons grown out of a tree (except they are not edible). The folks would cut them in half, clean out the inside, and let them dry in the sun so that they would become the consistency of wood.

Every child in my village was poor; but I was worse off—most of them had at least one parent present. When I became aware of my surroundings, I realized I didn't have my father or mother around me. My father, who was no help to me, had children all over Haiti. He traveled from very far to take advantage of young, innocent women; and he abandoned Maman while she was still pregnant with me. I learned that my mother left me when I was only nine months old. The neighbors told me Maman suffered very much because she was so poor. One morning she decided to venture to the city, Port-au-Prince, to discover what life had in store for her—and to end a lifetime of poverty. She left me behind with a lady named Betila. They told me Maman had planned to send for me as soon as she could, but life in the city was tough and things didn't turn out the way she expected. It would be a long time before she could send for me.

As soon as Maman took off, I became ill. Many deadly diseases vowed to end my existence so much so that I often lost all my strength. My unhealthy diet, which mostly consisted of breadfruit, added to my misery. Do you know what breadfruit is? It looks like pineapples on the outside but tastes like extra tough potatoes. My already weak digestive system could not process this much starch; but since I survived by eating breadfruit night and day, my stomach was always bloated. I had constant indigestion, and parasites were eating me alive.

I wanted to give up many times because my body was so weak, but my spirit refused to do so. It wanted me to stay in the ring and fight one more battle. I spent most of my time during the day sitting on a dirt floor fanning flies off my face; and at night, I shooed away the mosquitoes. I was so alone. There were times when I wondered whether I had been brought to this earth by a spirit who had then abandoned me.

Every day I cried for my mother's help. I heard that I had a sister and a brother in the City with Maman. I wanted to be close to my family. Perhaps then I could be touched, even held. Psychologists tell us that children who are not cuddled, held, and touched have a tendency to shrink and die early. I desperately needed some type of affection.

The Cynical Predictions Of The Lay Fortune Tellers

Yes, I suffered the blows of poverty; and I endured the pain of sickness and loneliness—but the highest mountain I had to climb was dealing with the teasing and ridiculing of the people in the village. They made fun of my swollen tummy and my skeletal body. Some villagers belittled me. They called me Kokobay and Souyan. Kokobay is an actual Creole word, which means crippled. I found out that there was an actual person named Souyan. He was crippled with a flat behind. He, too, had to put up with teasing and name-calling.

When the strong tropical wind blew in the village, I ran and braced my feeble body against trees in order to avoid being blown away. My condition had deteriorated so much that some people predicted I would not survive to adulthood. They even told me so, but God proved them wrong. I made it. Do you remember the cigarette commercial for Virginia Slims? That's the way I feel: I have come a long way baby!

What I went through is only my experience. While my family was living on the edge, there were those living a good life. Some were driving expensive cars, living in hilltop mansions, and traveling the world. These people can't identify with my story, but they are not the majority.

What about you? How long have you traveled to get where you are today? Where did you start in life? Some people, particularly Haitians, often ask if I'm embarrassed to share so much of my early life with strangers. Why should I be embarrassed? It doesn't matter where you start; what matters is where you finish. Society does not evaluate me based on my past. A Fortune 500 company never looks at my past before hiring me to speak to their employees. Instead, they hire me because of what I have accomplished. It is who I am today that earns me respect and admiration. Regardless of where we start—whether it's the ghetto or a tiny village in Haiti—with a strong vision, solid goals, and a sense of direction, we can have a great finish. Where we come from is not as relevant as where we are going. When I stand on a platform staring at three thousand souls waiting for me to boost their batteries, to touch their souls—they are interested in one thing: what I can offer them in that moment!

Been There, Done That And Got The T-Shirt

I am not looking for pity. I just want to illustrate that I am not sitting on a mountaintop preaching to the masses. When I say, "It doesn't matter where you start, what matters is where you finish," I am speaking with conviction. I've been there—poverty-stricken, hungry, tired, and diseased. I know that no condition is ever permanent. My goal is to convince you that your world is limitless—that it is important to remember your past but that it should never stop you from reaching for the top. Your future has very little to do with your past unless you think so. What matters most is not your current position. Hard work and preparation can unlock the doors of your future regardless of where you are or where you started.

Your starting point is just a way of getting in the door; it's your launching pad, although it has nothing to do with how high you can fly. If you want to have a great finish, you must decide now to make it happen. My greatest concern is that people look at where they start, and from there they determine there is no way to ever accomplish anything significant. There is no dead-end! We decide what roads to take, what paths to pursue.

Take Charge Of Your Life

Have you ever heard someone say life is unfair? I disagree. I think life is very fair; however, many of us are unfair to life. We are all endowed with the power to choose. Whether you are rich or poor, black or white, pretty or ugly, life gives you twenty-four hours in a day. It's up to you to choose how you spend those hours. You can either cruise on automatic pilot wasting your hours, or you can decide to study, plan, and prepare for tomorrow. The choice is yours; but whatever you do, you must be prepared to face the consequences.

What did you do yesterday with your hours? What about today? What specific step will you take to make sure you are becoming the kind of person you want to be? When you make empowering choices, you acquire a sense of control. Psychologists call this the "locus of control." This means having enough of a sense of control and confidence to move forward. My guess is that you either have some degree of control or you are totally in control. How do I know? Without being somewhat in control of your life, you would never have chosen to read this book. I hope you make another choice—to read all the chapters.

Will your life change because of this book? I would never make such claim, but here is what I know for sure: If you continue to make choices like this, they will all come together to create the big picture. After a speaking engagement, my audience always asks me questions about how I got to where I am. I don't have a logical answer to that question. Who I am today is not the result of a single event; rather, it's a culmination of the choices I made in the past. It's the way I chose to spend my twenty-four hours. Today you have the power to make several choices. My question to you is this: Will those choices give you an advantage for the future?

Exercise

Think for a moment about what you did yesterday. Now think about the choices you made today.

Did these choices help you become a better person or ensure you will live a better life?

1) Write down the wrong choices you made yesterday—the way you responded to a situation or the action you took.

2) Ask yourself: What better way could I have handled the situation that would make me feel a better person today?

3) Are the actions I took yesterday bringing me closer to or farther away from my goals?

4) Now write down the right and positive choices you made.

5) Describe how you feel about those good choices.

Take Control NOW To Better Your Tomorrow

Write down what you will do now to right the wrongs of yesterday.

There is nothing you can do to erase yesterday's mistakes. Life is not like a computer. There are no delete buttons. It makes no sense beating yourself up. Get over it! You only have control over your tomorrow. The best way to redeem yourself is to right the wrongs of yesterday or the last hour NOW.

Remember, our choices define who we are. Make the right choices, and you'll be on your way to your own personal success.

If You Don't Have A Target, You Can't Aim

When I ask most people about their vision or goals (such as where they will be five or ten years from now), they usually roll their eyes and blink a few times, but don't answer. I know that feeling; I was there. For years I was constantly searching for what I wanted to do with my life. Like I said before, although I have never met you, there is one thing I know for sure about you: You, too, are constantly looking and searching or you wouldn't be reading this now. We share a kindred spirit. Congratulations!

Everyone should have a dream about what he or she eventually wants to do in life. I'll never forget the day I met a very impressive young man by the name of Wesley Madhere, II. I went to a restaurant for dinner with some friends. Wesley was our waiter for the evening. He served us as if he owned the restaurant. He had a pleasant and pleasing smile on his face, and he carried himself like a winner. He gave us a true dining experience. We were really impressed!

Later, during a casual conversation with Wesley, we discovered a man who had an extraordinary vision for his future. We were totally blown away when Wesley excitedly painted a picture of his tomorrow. He was precise and confident. We were so excited about his dream that we wanted to take the trip with him. What vision!

At the time we met Wesley, he was a student working on a degree in business administration. His main goal was to open a restaurant. He already had a partner picked out. He told us how his partner was an excellent chef working toward a culinary degree. I'm certain Wesley will have no problem convincing a bank to loan him the money he needs to open his restaurant. Why? One reason is he has a well thought out plan. Second, he's passionate about his dreams. Wesley confirmed to me what I knew all along: A burning desire and a solid strategy are the prerequisites for success. Nothing significant has ever happened without solid strategies. Living is like being in a war. If you don't have calculated plans for your battles, you will lose every single one of them. I am confident that, one day, Wesley's dream of owning one of the finest restaurants in town will materialize, if he doesn't allow others to steal his dream. Could I say the same thing about you if you shared your plans with me? If your answer is no, it's time for you to do some serious thinking.

When You Know It And Feel It, Help Will Come

The first requirement of getting what you want in life is to know precisely what it is that you want. Leaders know this. They know that they must know and communicate their vision to the people looking up to them. In the past, I have worked with managers who came in to work every week and began shuffling procedures and people around; but we had no clue what their objectives were. I am sure they knew, but they didn't take time to communicate it. No one will be ready to assist you unless he or she knows and understands where you are heading; people will help you once they see your vision.

Many people have helped me as my career has progressed. Ed Primeau with *Primeau Productions* spent a whole day out of his busy schedule to assist me in putting together my demo video for my keynote presentations. It would have cost me thousands of dollars to get that kind of help, but Ed didn't charge me anything. I was having dinner with Ed later and I asked him why he didn't charge me. He told me he felt like Barry Gordy at Motown. Ed said, "I see your plans for the future and I get excited. I feel like I've discovered an incredible talent with sound plans to be a successful, professional speaker." He went on to tell me that every now and then he loves to step into someone's life and make a difference. "It was your turn," Ed said. Wow! Ed saw my vision—my burning desire. It is my hope that you too will have a burning desire that drives you to take action.

By now I am positive you are convinced of your need to draw a map for your future—about setting goals if you don't already have them in place. In the absence of goals and a sense of direction, you may be cruising the highways of life getting excellent mileage and enjoying smooth roads. However, because you don't know where you are heading, you end up burning all your fuel until you find yourself on the side of the road. If I asked you right now where you are going or what your vision is, could you tell me the answer like Wesley could? If you can't answer that question, it's time to sit down and do some soul searching. The reality is you are going somewhere. It may not be where you want to go, but your car is in motion. Decide now to take control; start planning now.

Exercise

Write out your map of where you want your life to go in the next 5 to 10 years. Don't hold anything back.

How did you do with the previous exercise? Was it easy, or did you struggle? If you struggled, don't despair; I've had many people say to me, "But I don't know what I want to do with my life. How can I draw a map when I don't know my passion?" Let me share with you some strategies to help find your passion.

How To Discover What You Were Born To Do

What are you passionate about? Very few people can answer that question. I know that for many years it was hard for me to even think about my passion. Yet, all along it was with me. What you were born to do is right there in front of your face, but you are too close to see it. It's very hard to enjoy the scenery when you are in it. There are those who say, "I don't have a passion," or "I wasn't born to do anything." Wrong. Everyone born on this earth has a role in some capacity.

In Africa, there is a village in a country named Burkina Fasso (ber keen ah fasso). When a woman is pregnant there, the village elders perform a ritual. First they put the woman into a trance. Then they channel the baby's voice through the woman in order for the baby to reveal its purpose. Once they find out the baby's purpose, they groom the child in a way that will lead him or her to live according to his or her purpose.

Wouldn't it be nice if someone came to you when you were a child and told you exactly what you were born to do? Yes, but of course it doesn't happen this way. No, it's up to you to discover your role, your passion; this is your job. You have to discover it yourself.

Here are some thoughts to keep in mind as you set about discovering your purpose:

- Keep it simple. Ask yourself what you like to do, what intrigues you, what you can lose yourself in.

- Don't expect a quick answer. It may take you a long time to find your purpose, but it is out there.

- Trust yourself. How will you know when you have found your purpose? When deep inside yourself you feel that you are making a difference in the lives of others, you have probably come in contact with your passion.

- A passion isn't solely personal. Your passion may get you excited, but it should also help others. When you help others solve their problems and enrich their lives, you are well on the way to discovering your passion.

- Work feels like play. Finally, when you can't tell whether you are working or playing you know that's your passion. Speaking and writing are what juice me up. That is the way I offer the world my talents and skills—the way I make a contribution. I can be on the computer at one o'clock in the morning working but I don't even feel like I am working. I go to bed and wake up in the morning thinking about my passion—the ways I can help my listeners improve their lives. My conversations always tend to turn to speaking. Some of my friends can't understand why I work so hard. How could they? It's hard to imagine. You've got to experience it.

Your WHY Is More Important Than Your How

> *"If we have our own why of life, we shall*
> *get along with almost any how..."*—Friedrich Nietzsche

Until you know with certainty that you are on a mission to contribute to the human race, you will always have a void in your life.

The whole universe is like one big domino effect. MY life is better when YOU decide to live on purpose, and vice versa. That's what the philosopher Friedrich Nietzsche calls your WHY. Purpose is the high-octane fuel that revs up your internal engines. So, what is your why? What drives you to want to do what you do?

Many years ago, I found an exercise that helped me discover my WHY. After I decided to become a motivational speaker, I wanted to know whether I had chosen the right path for my life. I had already tried my hands at many other things, but I discovered that I was chasing success because of the money it would bring me. All along my motive was in the wrong place. Money is a byproduct of the value we provide to society. One can never experience enduring success if money is the WHY. Simply put, success comes when it is other-oriented rather than self-oriented. Coincidentally, money flows in abundance when we set out to make life better for others.

Believe me, I don't have problems with money. Money is a good thing. It affords me the ability to have a good life and to help others. I've heard it said that the best way to help the poor is not to be one of them. However, money plays a weird game sometimes. It goes to the people who are busy doing what they are passionate about. It seems as though the more you focus on money, the more money runs away from you.

Here Is How You Can Begin To Explore Your Passion

Take time out of your crowded schedule to do the exercise I am about to recommend. Keep in mind that if you want to make sure your condition is not permanent, you must take time now to strategize for the future. Do you agree? Okay.

- Sit down in a quiet place with a pad and pen. Draw three columns on a blank page. Divide your age into three age ranges and place the three figures, one on each column. For example, if you were 30 years old, you would have a column from your birth to age 10, another from age 10 to 20, and the final from age 20 to 30.

- Next, write down things you have done during each age range. Write down as much as you can, even if some events appear to be insignificant to you.

- Now study what you have written. Attempt to find out what the common denominator is about you in all the three segments. In other words, what are some of the activities that occurred over and over throughout your life?

When I did this exercise, I discovered there was a common thread in all the things I did as a child. I found that I was always trying to entertain or inspire an audience. According to all my activities, I was supposed to be an encourager. There is no accident. If you are stuck with this exercise and you don't seem to be able to find your life's patterns, ask your parents and friends what common threads they see in you.

Here's another way to find your WHY: If you had just won the lottery and money was not an issue, what kind of work would you do for free? The answer to that question is where your passion lies. I am convinced that what you were born to do and who you were born to be is calling you every day. You have to listen to that still, quiet voice inside of you.

Hope Is The Light That Shines At The End Of The Tunnel

As I travel the country giving motivational speeches to thousands, I am often asked how I found the courage to press on in the face of such overwhelming odds. Once a lady asked me, "What is your secret?" I don't have a secret. It's like a combination lock. It took putting all the numbers in the right order. One day I dug deep inside of me to find the one thing that enabled me to rise above my challenges, and I found one thing that stood out. It may sound trite, yet it is exactly what brought me this far. My secret is one word. It may be simplistic to you, but I urge you not to dismiss it. It is called HOPE.

When I was lonely and isolated in the village, somehow I knew that things were going to get better someday. In the absence of hope—a positive expectancy—it's easy to give up the fight. You have to be able to see the light at the end of the tunnel—to know that *No Condition is Permanent!*. Many years ago a group of researchers conducted a study with rats. They put one group in a pool of water. After a couple minutes, they rescued them. The researchers then put the rats in the pool a second time but left them in longer. After the fifth try, they watched the rats struggle for over one hour without sinking. They then tried the experiment with another group of rats without rescuing them at all. After about just ten minutes, the second group of rats started sinking below the water. They gave up very fast. Why did the second group of rats drop dead while the first paddled the water with courage? One reason is that the second group didn't know that there was a possibility of being rescued. They had no hope. Their condition appeared to be permanent.

It doesn't matter what you are facing today in your life: your condition is not permanent! It may appear to be so, but your help is coming. Are you trying to accomplish something that is taking a long time and the results are not coming in? That's called life. Nothing is easy. The old adage says if it's worth having, it's worth fighting for. Stay in the race just a little longer. Provide greater value than expected and give your best every time. It is that kind of hopeful attitude that can light up your dark moments and sustain you in the fight.

Exercise

Imagine for a moment that you spent every penny you owned and charged your credit cards to the limit to open a business. It's your passion. However, some friends and family members downplay your idea. They disapprove of your decision to go into business. Some tell you directly while others are hypocritical.

Six months into the business, you are not even making enough money to pay the rent! You start knocking on doors in an attempt to find new customers. You make calls all day. You leave messages, but no one bothers to return your calls. You face nothing but rejection and deception. You submit one proposal after another to no avail. You are totally exhausted from working too many hours. Except for a couple of loyal friends, every one seems to desert you. Then there are those who are talking behind your back saying, "I told her! But she wouldn't listen," or "I told him, but he wouldn't listen." According to statistics, it seems as though you are wasting your time.

Question: How would you feel, or what would you do?
Now that you have expressed your feelings, let me shine some light in your window. One day you get home. You are drained, sleepy and beat down. All you want to do is to throw yourself on the bed and sob. You check your mail and find a letter from a client who read your proposal some time ago. Fortunately, it's a Fortune 500 company. They are bringing suppliers on board, and you are one of their choices. According to the letter, they want to sign a contract with you worth one hundred thousand dollars. After six months, if they like your performance, they will refer you to five other companies. They also promise to provide you with all the right support to ensure your success. That means that in one year you will be running a company worth half a million dollars! According to your business plan, your net profit will be one hundred fifty thousand dollars.

Question: Describe how you would feel after reading that letter. Would you hire the friends and family members who didn't think much of your idea?
Did you get excited and full of energy when you heard that news? Where did you find the energy you now have when less than ten minutes ago you were so drained and exhausted? Answer: You always had it! You just needed to tap into it. That energy is HOPE! This is my whole point. A clear and vivid vision of a hopeful future will wake you up bright and early in the morning full of passion, motivation and energy. No matter how dim your future looks to others, with hope, you will always have a gigantic spotlight in it. The lesson? See your future in a three-dimensional view. Smell

it, touch it, live it everyday and be nuts about it. Believe me, I can tell you from personal experience that this is the cure for a stressful and depressing day.

Everyone Has A Village

I believe we are all living in a village. Perhaps yours is not without electricity, plumbing, and medical care; but your family, your circle of friends, and your work environment are all villages. There may be those in your village who don't think much of you, just like there were in my village. They sometimes belittle you and they try to put you down. You might even have some jealous people in your village. You may feel unappreciated for your contributions.

Perhaps you are not starving for food in your village, but you may be starving for love, affection, and recognition. How do you deal with that?

• Take control.

• Quit focusing externally.

• Look within for your happiness.

What people think about you is just their opinion; but what you think about yourself is your reality. Dare to hope; you will prevail.

We bemoan, groan, and complain about our present status even though we are given the power to do something about it. Considering where I started in life, it's almost a miracle for me to be where I am today. Not long ago I took a trip back to my village. The folks looked at me with amazement in their eyes. They told me, "Ti bête gan sang (tee bet gahn sahn)." It's a Creole proverb which means as long as there is blood running trough the veins, there is hope. You and I have no control over external situations in life, but we have a choice as to how we interpret them—we can always rely on HOPE.

Hope is like an internal pilot light. As long as that tiny light is alive inside of you, you will bear your cross with grace and elegance. Without it, darkness will surround you, and despair will envelop you. That is why so many people end their lives. They believe their condition is permanent. For many of you, no matter what you are going through at this moment, you are not going to be paddling in the water for too much longer. Your rescue team is on the way. You may not see it now, but it's closer than you might imagine. Like Henry David Thoreau said, "I have learned this at least by my experiment—that if one advances confidently in the direction of his dreams and endeavors to live the life which he has imagined, he will meet with a success unexpected in common hours."

CHAPTER TWO

Believe
When Others Doubt!

Believe
When Others Doubt!

∞

*"Keep away from people who try to belittle your ambitions.
Small people always do that, but the really great make you
feel that you, too, can become great."*— Mark Twain

There are times when you will come up with a great idea
that you know and believe is a good one. If the idea makes
enough sense, some people will become excited and want
to help you make it a reality by investing their time or money. Not
everybody will rally behind you. In fact, there are those who will
probably ridicule you. They will talk negatively about you behind
your back and try to discourage you. They may even suggest that
you're borderline crazy.

There are doubters to every new idea. You must not let these
doubters stop you from pressing on. They are not qualified to be
your fortuneteller; they do not have all the answers. Can you overcome these doubters? Yes. You must simply believe in yourself
and in your own abilities. It's nice if others believe in you, of
course. In fact, that's great oxygen for your soul; but ultimately it's
your own internal fuel of belief that must keep you going.

Many of my fellow villagers gave up on me. They didn't think
I was going to survive. Their cynical predictions loomed over me
throughout my childhood. All around me were messengers telling
me that I would not long survive—that my life would be brief and
painful. Some even said that I would never—*could* never—

accomplish anything worthwhile before I died. According to these doubters, for me to even try to achieve something worthwhile would be pointless—to believe otherwise would be foolish.

Those were their words and beliefs. I had my own internal beliefs—that my life would not only continue, but it would also get much better. I predicted for myself a better life. I saw my own light at the end of the tunnel. I believed a tide would one day come in to lift my boat.

Have others ever treated you the same way? Have you ever encountered that kind of fatal cynicism expressed by people in your village, be they work colleagues, family members, or friends? Have you, whether openly or by implication, been told that you did not matter and never would? Have you ever been told that you should just give up and live out your remaining days in miserable, meager gratitude? Come on! Maybe it wasn't a direct assault on your self-esteem, but more than likely you have had a similar experience. If you haven't, trust me, you will. Coming face to face with—and overcoming—doubters is one way to grow in life, and it's what this chapter is all about.

Believe In Yourself

When I decided motivational speaking was my calling, I had little confidence I would succeed in the speaking arena. My English was very poor, I had few resources, financial or otherwise, and I didn't know how to relate to American audiences. Because I came from a different culture, I thought it would be hard for me to make a connection with my listeners. The odds were definitely against me, and I was afraid.

Not only did I have my own doubts; but also others tried to discourage me. Some told me straight out that I was wasting my time. Others were more polite; they didn't tell me with their words, but their attitudes spoke loud and clear. Even some of my friends weren't supportive. One friend tried to discourage me by saying he thought I lacked the education necessary to become a motivational speaker. "You don't even have a degree," he told me. My friend believed a degree would open some closed doors for me. Little did he know that I had my own Ph.D. I worked on it for years. My thesis was on the stuff success is made of. My school was the University of Hard Knocks. My Ph.D is P = persistence, H = Hope, and D = dreams. With such a degree, I can kick open any closed door!

Receiving criticism or other negative input from colleagues or acquaintances is one thing, but what about when the criticism comes from someone you had expected to encourage and support you? Ouch! It hurts! Doesn't it?

Receiving criticism from someone who we believed would support us is when our belief in ourselves is most sorely tested. Sometimes there will be no one else in the world to believe in you, or to give you accolades; no one to have faith in your ability to exceed expectations, to accomplish something of great worth and importance. In these cases you will need your own faith and courage to brave the storms. You must go beyond the mean-spirited predictions of others. No one but you knows what you are capable of. Even when those around you are ready to give up, you must stand still and know you will succeed.

Here Are Some Specific Ways To Keep The Faith You Have In Yourself Alive And Kicking:

- **Refuse to let friends push their agenda on you.** Only I know what's possible in my life; my friends don't know what I'm ultimately capable of doing. This project is an example. It has always been a dream of mine to write a book. You are holding my dream in your hands! With a little ambition and self-sacrifice, you can go a long way.

- **Know that not everyone will be supportive of your ideas and plans.** Why is it that everyone doesn't rally behind us to help us materialize our dreams? I am as bewildered as you are on that question. Here is what I do know: don't let doubters stop you; let them become one of the motivating factors to help propel you toward your ambitions.

- **Conquer your own doubts.** When I was considering becoming a motivational speaker, I had to affirm to myself over and over that I could succeed. I mustered all my courage to take action, and I went for my dream in spite of my fears, doubts, and concerns about what others were thinking about me.

- **Realize that success takes time.** When Christopher Columbus was sailing on the seas, his crew continually asked him to give up. Each time they went to Christopher, he pulled out his binoculars and looked for something to convince his boat mates that land and their success were close. One morning he finally screamed from the top of his lungs when he saw some birds. Why? The birds were evidence that there was land ahead. What about you? Are you close to getting your breakthrough? How much time, energy, and money have you invested in your endeavor so far?

To keep your dream alive, your faith in yourself must burn deep within you. I think of this burning belief as the lighthouse that guides you to your destination. When opportunity presents itself like fuel to a fire, it is the passion that ignites your most stunning accomplishments, your most magical moments. I could never have become who I am today without that burning faith in myself. I could never have escaped my village. I would have died young, just as everyone thought.

Stay True To Yourself

A few years ago when I was new to the speaking industry, I learned that I needed a demo video to promote myself to corporate clients. I didn't have the money to hire a video production company, so I had to come up with a creative way to get the video made. Here's what happened.

I was working as a doorman for the Renaissance Waverly Hotel in Atlanta, Georgia. That's how I got to know the general manager, Herman Gammiter, and the director of catering, Mary Jo Ferrazza. Mr. Gammiter is such an exceptional man. He heard my

"No Condition is Permanent!" presentation at the Vinnings Rotary Club, of which he is a very active member. He was impressed. Next thing I know, he went and asked the human resources director to have me speak to all the hotel employees. You may not know Mr. Gammiter, but that says a lot about who he is. Wouldn't you be glad if your boss supported your deepest dreams and aspirations? I bet you would be more productive at work, too.

After hearing me speak at the hotel, Mary Jo became a big fan. She was crazy about me and was convinced that I had enough talent to make it in the speaking arena. She saw the best in me and she took every opportunity to point it out to me and to others. I was certainly moved by the way she embraced my dream. So, I went to both Herman and to Mary Jo with a win-win deal. I asked them to provide me with the food, room, and drinks needed to host a speaker's showcase. In return, the speakers would provide training in sales, customer service, and management techniques for the hotel.

Next, the other speakers and I each chipped in the money required to do a two-camera video shoot. Then we invited anybody and everybody as an audience, as we needed warm bodies to respond to our presentations. I went around to the local bookstores and restaurants asking for door prizes in order to encourage attendance. I got commitments from almost everyone I approached. Man, I was on a roll!

After a long and tiring three months of preparation and planning, the showcase became a reality, and my demo video was born. It was a labor of love! That video allowed me to present in front of over two thousand members of the National Speakers Association. As you can imagine, I was very proud of my work!

There is the general belief in the speaking arena that if you don't have a demo video, you must not be serious about speaking. I went from talking and dreaming about becoming a professional speaker to actually becoming one! My dreams had become reality. The fact that I was still a doorman, living off my tips, never made me lose confidence in the direction I was heading! In fact, it was a stepping-stone to my success.

Watch Out For Dream Busters!

Once I finished editing my video, I began showing it around to others. Although I believe we are our own best coaches, I thought a little feedback would do me a lot of good. Yet, there was something else going on, too: I wanted to impress my friends; I was looking for approval. I went to one family member expecting him to give me some kudos, as well as a little encouragement. Well, I guessed wrong!

The moment I started talking about my struggle with diseases in my village in Haiti, he sarcastically chuckled. He told me that he was shocked to hear me tell such a big "lie," that I had never had that kind of life. He also suggested I give up professional speaking altogether. As if that wasn't bad enough, his wife was 100 percent behind him. They were both laughing at my dream.

I was in shock. I hadn't expected such a negative reaction. My story is authentic. When I was going through those very difficult times in my life in the village, this guy didn't know me then. Even my own mother, sister, and brother were not there with me. They remembered my swollen tummy and my bouts with constant indigestion after I arrived in the City. I only came to know him when I was in my twenties.

Although the shock was startling, I did learn something that night. I left the gentleman's house with a resolution to be careful with whom I shared my goals, dreams, and aspirations. I learned, too, that people view my story through the story of their life. Part of their reaction, I now believe, was due to the fact that in our culture one does not go into public and reveal his or her poverty-stricken past. To them, what I was saying reflected their past even though they didn't have things nearly as bad as I did. My close family, in general, was not happy at first when I started sharing my story. However, they didn't try to burst my bubble either.

Today, I totally forgive the man and his wife for their lack of understanding that night. I am sure they didn't realize what their remarks did to my self-confidence. While they are good people with good intentions, unfortunately it came to a point where I stopped sharing my dreams with them.

Build—Don't Destroy

I share this story with you not because I resent them. I simply want to make you aware of how others can kill your dream in a heartbeat. It also illustrates that many times the dream busters are good people who mean well. We should not try to get even with them or resent them, because they don't know what they are doing. I know some act out of pure jealousy; they destroy our dreams on purpose. However, many tend to mean well. Whatever the case, you can't let someone else's ignorance destroy you. Move on!

You can spend ten to twenty years building a dream that a negative person can destroy in one minute. Not long ago, I witnessed a team of men demolishing a building. The job was done in no time. I asked the man in charge about what it would take to rebuild. His answer didn't surprise me. He said to me the demolishers have very low skills; their specialty is to demolish—to tear apart. He went on to tell me it's a lot easier to find excellent destroyers than decent builders. Rebuilding takes much more time and talent.

Beware. You might be surrounded by destroyers who abuse you and tear you apart with such finesse that you don't notice it. What's remarkable about some destroyers is that they may not even realize what they are doing—they're simply creatures of habit. Yet, if you pay close attention, you will notice their intention. They have a way of talking you out of your calling. Don't you know people like this? They are on a mission to take you to the gutters with them.

The truth is, every now and then we can all get into a destroying mood. Every day I check myself to make sure that I am not stepping on someone else's dream. I urge you to do the same. When others trust and value you enough to share their goals and dreams with you, they are looking for encouragement. They want a boost. Even when you think their idea does not make sense to you, you should not dismiss it too quickly. Perhaps you can sleep on it a little until you can offer a way to improve upon it. Remember, it's not what you say; it's how you say it. For those of you who don't know how to offer your advice without offending others, I strongly suggest that you read *How to Win Friends and Influence People* by Dale Carnegie.

Seek Advice From Trusted Advisors

I know when I give my best and when I fail to measure up. Although we can sometimes be too harsh on ourselves, I truly understand my success does not come from what others believe or think about me; it's what I believe. I don't mean to be arrogant by pretending that I know everything. Au contraire, I constantly seek advice. Yet when I seek feedback, I go to TRUSTED ADVISORS—people who have my best interests at heart. My trusted advisors are those who truly want to see me succeed—they are, in effect, my cheerleaders and coaches. They can be brutally honest with me without crushing my ego because I know they care.

Cavet Robert, the founder of the National Speakers Association, put it best when he said, "No one cares how much you know until they know how much you care." You should seek advice and feedback from people who care about you. I am very fortunate to be surrounded by such people. I remember when I started speaking. Shirley Garrett got out of bed before 6:00 a.m. to listen to and evaluate my presentation. I know Shirley cares. She is a phenomenal speaker herself and she genuinely wants me to succeed. My great speaker-friend and mentor Myra McElhaney is the person I call from my hotel room before a speech to ask for last minute advice. Myra knows how to bring out the best in me. Her advice is always on target, and I know she cares.

Get A Mentor Now

Whether you work for somebody else or for yourself, if you are serious about success, you need a mentor, someone who has achieved the kind of success you are after. When you need feed-back, you can't go to a destroyer to help build your future. You must have an advisory board off which to bounce your ideas. Your board does not have to be as formal as that of a Fortune 500 company. Myra is one of my best board members even though she doesn't have a formal title as board member of Village Hero, Inc.

Exercise

- Who has served as your mentor in the past?

- How successful was this relationship? What could you have done to make it better?

- Now make a list of people who might serve as a mentor or a "board of directors" for you today? (Hold on to this list. We will discuss how best to use it in a minute.)

By the way, do you need a board if your business is very small? You bet. Even if you don't have a business at all, you still need an advisory board. In addition to providing ideas and guidance, they will hold you accountable for your success. You should have at least five or more great friends you can rely on for feedback on your ideas. Ultimately, you are the judge. You know best, but just like the great Jewish King Solomon said, "As iron sharpens iron, so a man sharpens the countenance of his friend."

How To Choose And Work With Mentors

Remember I asked you to hold on to your list of potential mentors. Pull it out! Here are three simple steps to choosing a mentor.

1) Ask

Rosita Perez is one of the most outstanding and respected speak-ers in the world. Watching her on stage is like watching Michelangelo carving a masterpiece. Rosita's message has touched and changed lives the world over. One day I called Rosita and asked for her advice. To my surprise, she invited me to spend a day with her at her Florida home. On that day, I felt like I was in the presence of an angel. I walked away empowered to reach my dreams. How did I get to spend a day with the master? I asked. Sometimes we have to send our ego on a vacation and ask for help.

The Bible says, *"Ask and you shall receive."* I must admit I have a real problem asking for help. My ego often gets in the way. Part of it is because of my background. Asking was almost a sin when I was a kid. I had no idea it would be so easy to meet with Rosita. I remember her telling me that anybody could get a day with her; he or she simply has to ask.

All the help you and I need is right there for us if we ask. I am getting a lot better now at asking for advice. When I need someone's time, I ask for it. When we ask, we have nothing to lose and everything to gain. I probably could write a whole chapter on asking. For now all you need to know is to ask courteously. Don't feel like anyone is obligated to assist you. In fact, the only hands you can absolutely depend on to always be there for you are the ones hanging by your side. Any other help is a privilege. So, ask someone to mentor you…to be your board member today.

2) *Choose someone who is living your dream.*
When you are thirsty, you should never go a dry well. Your mentor should not be a cute person whose face you enjoy watching. He should have knowledge and experience in your field. She should have enough energy to boost your battery.

3) *Make sure you know the person cares about your success.*
Nothing is more devastating than taking advice from someone who has a hidden agenda. There are people who are very comfortable giving you advice as long as you are one level below them. As soon as you move up one rung of the ladder ahead of them, they get jealous. They may not say or admit this, but you will feel it. So, make sure you know the person cares about your success.

What To Do Once You Find A Mentor

1) Be considerate of the person's time.

Everyone is busy. We are always juggling many balls. To a productive and successful person, every hour is precious. Show up on time and be prepared. Be utterly grateful that your mentor has agreed to spend time with you no matter how short.

2) Ask specific questions.

Don't go to your mentor and say, "I need help." He or she is not psychic. You must articulate exactly what areas in your life or business require help. Before you meet with your mentor, write down your questions. Also, remember to ask open-ended questions like "How would you handle this situation if you were me?"

3) Listen, listen, listen.

It's amazing how someone asks for advice but then ends up doing all the talking. If we knew what to do in the first place, we wouldn't have had to ask. When I ask, I zip it up and listen. We can only learn when we are listening and observing, not when we are talking. Everyone loves to talk about his or her accomplishments. Fire up the question, listen, and take copious notes.

4) Follow through.

If you want to frustrate your mentor, take his or her advice and do nothing with it. Success results from follow through. Your mentor or board member's gift to you is his or her advice. When you apply the gift, you actually give him or her a gift back. No matter what line of work you are in, if you make a solid commitment to follow through, your future is virtually unlimited.

5) Be grateful—send a little gift.

A person can say 'thank you' in more than a thousand ways. An attitude of gratitude is imperative. Occasionally, surprise your mentor with a small gift—a token of appreciation. Write a personal note to say thank you. Remember this: Your mentor/mentee relationship is like any other relationship. You must learn how to earn and keep the good will of the other person.

Let's Review

No condition is ever permanent. There are many things we can do to take our condition from permanent to temporary. I have shared with you what you can do to change your condition.

1) First you must whole-heartedly believe in your own ability. What others think is their opinion about you, but what you think about yourself is your reality. Whether you get all the support in the world or lots of criticism, you still can get ahead if you believe you can. Surround yourself with people who can encourage and support your dreams.

2) Choose someone who is living your dream.

3) Refuse to take feedback from others unless you know they sincerely care about your welfare.

Optimist International, an international, non-profit organization that promotes community involvement, has a creed that its members recite at the end of every meeting. Over the years, it has become my personal creed and I have committed it to memory. I share the creed with thousands. I am excited to have the opportunity to share it with you. It helps me to keep the things I share in this chapter with you in perspective. I hope it does the same for you. I also hope you take the time to reflect on the words. Please read it and feel free to share it with others, particularly with those who you suspect are destroyers. Enjoy the Creed and get ready for the next chapter.

Promise Yourself

To be so strong that nothing
can disturb your peace of mind.
To talk health, happiness and prosperity
to every person you meet.
To make all your friends feel
that there is something in them.
To look at the sunny side of everything
and make your optimism come true.
To think only of the best, to work only for the best
and to expect only the best.
To be just as enthusiastic about the success of others
as you are about your own.
To forget the mistakes of the past
and press on to the greater achievements of the future.
To wear a cheerful countenance at all times
and give every living creature you meet a smile.
To give so much time to the improvement of yourself
that you have no time to criticize others.
To be too large for worry, too noble for anger,
too strong for fear, and too happy
to permit the presence of trouble.

The Optimist Creed
From Optimist International

CHAPTER THREE

────────── ❦ ──────────

Learn To Love The Process; It's Precious!

Learn To Love The Process;
It's Precious!

"The secret success of every man who has ever been successful lies in the fact that he formed the habit of doing those things that failures don't like to do."—A. Jackson King

The mistress of ceremony introduced the first speaker. Ten minutes later, the second speaker made his way to the front of the room. He was just as good as the first. Then the third speaker topped the previous two—he was phenomenal! The thought of having to follow my three predecessors sent goose bumps up my spine. I had never given a speech before in my life! The idea of standing in front of people scared the daylights out of me, but the mistress of ceremony went on with the show! Now, it was my turn. I was about to give my icebreaker—the required seven-minute speech that serves as the rite of passage for new members of Toastmasters International. The subject is always easy— tell us about yourself.

The mistress of ceremony began with my introduction. Inside my head I screamed, "Oh, no! I'm not ready!" My heart began pounding like a galloping horse; my chest tightened; my knees buckled. The proverbial butterflies started flapping their wings inside my stomach. I looked at the exit door. I knew I had two choices: wait for my slow death in front of that podium, or bolt for the door. Does this sound familiar to you?

"...Ladies and gentlemen, let's welcome our fourth speaker for the evening…Rene Godefroy!" All eyes turned on me. I leapt out of my seat and hopped to the front of the room. The podium was my only comfort. I grabbed it and hid behind it. The room was quiet as my audience patiently waited to hear what I had to say. For a moment, I completely forgot who I was or where I was from. I unintentionally took a pregnant pause, which I later found out was the best thing to do. I then rattled off my speech at a hundred miles an hour. When a speaker is nervous, he or she tends to speak fast. Since my native language, Creole, is fast by nature, I tend to talk like I'm sprinting when I am nervous! Off I flew!

The good Lord helped me make it through my icebreaker. From the first word that came out of my mouth to the last, the audience paid rapt attention. They felt my pain. "Two minutes left," the timekeeper signaled me from the back of the room. "Uh…uh." I began to fill every second and minute with filler words. I closed with, "Thank you Madame Toastmaster," then headed to my seat to catch my breath.

As long as I live, I shall never forget that dramatic experience. I felt like a fool. I was embarrassed and felt awkward. Within three minutes of that presentation I had made just about every speaking mistake possible. I broke all the rules of public speaking. Thank God I had a very sympathetic audience that understood what I was going through.

Today, however, speaking is second nature for me. I am amazed at my ability to almost instantly connect with thousands of people. I no longer embarrass myself. My dream was to impact people at their very core—to make a difference in their lives. Now I am living that dream. It's all because I dared to face my fear and passionately persevered. What about you? Do you have talents that can enrich the lives of others? Are you afraid of stepping out because you might embarrass yourself, or others may laugh at you? You need to get over it, and I'm about to show you how!

Dare To Be Lousy

If your life is in neutral waiting for the right time to shift gears, you're in trouble. Why? Because there is never a right time. Now is the time to shift gears! You might say, "Well, I don't know where or how to start, or I'm not good enough to have the confidence to go for it." Guess what? I didn't have confidence when I gave my first Toastmasters speech. What you are actually saying is either you don't want to make a fool of yourself, or you want to start too big. Both of these negative thoughts must be overcome to move forward and to grow. Everything is a process. Every transformation requires incremental steps. Yes, you have to start somewhere, but I can guarantee you that you won't begin at the top.

This truth is universal. The people we admire in our lives gain our respect and admiration because they have spent years taking two steps forward and one step back. They eventually took enough steps to have the success work in their favor, but not every step was pleasant or positive. Along their journey, they experienced embarrassments, rejections, and disappointment. These successful people do not have magical powers, nor are they geniuses; but they did have the persistence to continue. Boil it all down and success is all about guts!

Let me give you another example about not starting at the top. Do you think the caterpillar one day says, "I am going to grow wings and take off?" No. It goes through a process of transformation. When I was a kid in the village, I was very impatient with the young coconut, mangos, and avocado trees; they took what seemed like forever to begin bearing fruit. Success is similar; it's all about patience and persistence. Hang in there and you will see the fruit.

Exercise:

- Think of a time when you were attempting something and then stopped along the way. Looking back, would it have benefited you to have kept on?

- What projects or processes are you involved with now that will require your continued persistence? Do you have what it takes to continue the journey no matter what?

Nature is replete with examples that teach us about patience and maturity. Those trees for which I could not wait to bear fruit taught me about patience. The other villagers rarely noticed the trees as they were growing (the process); but when the fruit on them was ripe, then they were noticed and envied by everyone. It's the same for you and me when we endure the hardships necessary to reach our goals. In a later chapter, I will expound on that; for now, let's talk about growth and staying power.

The Longer The Stronger

The trees that take years to mature tend to be around for ages. They survive severe weather conditions. Their roots are deep and strong. Even if you break their limbs, they will grow back again and again. That is why the furniture makers choose to make their furniture from wood that is exposed to tough weather conditions. These trees tend to be as hard as rocks. Now consider the vines that grow overnight on these trees. The vines also die overnight. The vines are weak because they have not endured. Doesn't that tell you something? Then why are you rushing? Reflect on what you are attempting to do, absorb yourself in the process, learn as you go, and relish the journey. This is the only way to grow strong. It's the way to move from being awkward and lousy to achieving mastery.

I certainly didn't start at the top. Today, those who have attended my presentations describe me as captivating, humorous, charismatic, and authentic; but I remember when I was ridiculously shy, even tongue-tied. The thought of being on stage gave me butterflies. I can also remember how poor my first few speeches were; but *No Condition is Permanent!*. Right? Right!

The process I went through in learning to become a professional speaker taught me things that money could never buy. I became a strong tree—one with deep roots. Since I entered the world of speaking, I have met many people I consider vines—they disappeared early in the process. Are you a hardy tree or a weakly vine? I will let you answer that question for yourself.

Success Takes Guts

The journey that brought me from agonizing poverty in a tiny village in Haiti to my life today has been a long one. Would I ever trade that kind of life for anything else? Never! Every turn, every twist has been my teacher. I learned that there are rewards in the process. Everything you see around you is the result of a process. First, it was a thought. Then it was an awkward attempt to materialize the thought. Finally, if persistence prevailed, that thought turned into action. However, the joy of accomplishment is not in the accomplishment itself; it's in the process.

This concept certainly isn't limited to me. Compelling leaders and celebrities come from rock bottom. Their failings, embarrassments, and disappointments along the way propel them to exciting victories. The journey to success is like watching a fantastic movie. You don't say, "I can't wait for the movie to end so that I can enjoy the story." No, instead you secretly wish the movie would never end. The process of watching the movie is what gives you joy and excitement. We should enjoy our journey just like we enjoy the movie.

What are your aspirations and ambitions? Are you afraid of being lousy, of being criticized by others? Think about it. The people at the very top of the ladder have slipped a few times on the rungs. They experienced every feeling you may be experiencing now, but they dared! In the school of life there is a teacher that is patient, caring, and very considerate. Others will laugh at you and give up on you when you fail, but that teacher will be with you every step of the way. He will give you another chance to try again and again. You have to attend his class in order to achieve massive success, regardless of your definition of success. What's that teacher's name? EXPERIENCE!

I know that my telling you to persevere is easy—that the difficulty is in the doing. So what if the whole world indeed laughs at you as you step out to make your dream come true. Who cares? The losers in life are those who never try anything! Whether you are working for a company or yourself, you have to sometimes try the unthinkable by stepping out. If you are not making mistakes, you are not taking enough risks, and if you are not taking enough risks, you are not making progress. You must occasionally get out of your comfort zone.

What's Next?

Successful people become very bored when there are no more mountains to climb—when victory is too easy and too predictable. Before 1989, the International Olympic committee prohibited the U.S. Olympic basketball team from playing with professional players. Other countries were allowed to do so, but America could only play with their best college players. That made it very difficult for America to bring home a gold medal.

In 1988, the U.S. team lost to the Soviet Union in the Olympic semifinal game in Seoul, South Korea, taking home the bronze medal. It was a terrible blow. Eight months later the rules were changed, and the committee lifted the ban on America. NBA players were allowed to play side by side with college players. In 1992, the Dream Team was born, and America demonstrated that she was the undisputed leader in basketball. Millions of people the world over were glued to their TV sets to watch the superstars. Among those who played that year were Larry Bird, Magic Johnson, Michael Jordan, Karl Malone, Scottie Pippen, David Robinson and John Stockton. Since then, America has never failed to win the gold medal in basketball.

However, the Dream Team's popularity began to decline. Why? Winning became too predictable. The viewers had nothing more to look forward to. They knew that the Dream Team would win—and they did—from one Olympic event to the next. How ironic! Americans used to find Olympic basketball boring because Team USA was sure to lose. Now they find Team USA boring because they are sure to win! In the absence of any reasonable challenge, the games became dull and uninteresting. The viewers didn't have any more mental mountains to climb with the players. Do you see my point? Without challenges, your life becomes a series of dull moments. As you manage your challenges—your crises, you become the kind of person others admire and want to be around.

The Thrills Are In The Challenges

Each little success along the way should be celebrated. The thrill of life is in between our successful moments. We can look forward to the challenges that life gives us. They make us stretch to a place we have never been before. They juice up our lives. Think about it, Bill Gates, as of now, is estimated to have 54 billion dollars. Just to give you a perspective of how rich he is, if he gave every American one million dollars today, he would not even spend half a billion of his 54 billion! Why is the man still working so hard? Is it for the money? It's very unlikely. Bill Gates, as well as countless other wealthy people, enjoys the challenges. It is the joy of the journey, the process that revs up their engines.

What challenges are you facing today? Write them down and ask yourself how you can turn them into fuel to rev up your success engine. Remember, creativity is the source of abundance.

I Bought Everything!

If I mentioned Pablo Picasso, Michelangelo, Leonardo Da Vinci, and Glenna Salsbury, would you recognize the names? They are masters. My guess is that you may recognize each of those names except for Glenna Salsbury. She is a wordsmith. Glenna can connect with your emotions—your right brain—even if you are a total stranger to her. She uses words to paint vivid and colorful pictures in the mind of her listeners. Can you tell by now that Glenna is a speaker and writer?

On November 17, 2001, they all came to see Glenna. Some were accomplished speakers; others were aspiring speakers; but they all knew it would be a terrible mistake to miss being in the presence of such a master. We were all members of the National Speakers Association (NSA) of Georgia. Those who had not heard her before were in for a treat, and those of us who had seen and heard her didn't want to let another opportunity pass.

Most of us in the room were teachers. We travel the country to impact lives. However, that morning at the NSA Georgia, we were all attentive students. Have you ever been in the presence of someone who is highly captivating and charismatic—someone on whose every word you hung? That is how I felt about Glenna Salsbury. I wanted more. Glenna painted an incredible picture in my mind, using stories as her brush, and words as the fiber of her brush. Have you ever had an experience when you said, "Aha!"? All of us in that room that day had that experience. Glenna brought more meaning and significance to our calling in life. The master's hands had touched me, as they had touched everyone else in the room. That day I bought all of her learning materials. It was the only time I had ever bought everything from another speaker.

How is it that one human being can captivate the heart and soul of another with only his or her words? Is it an innate gift? No .One of the greatest communicators of civilization, if not the greatest, was the Greek philosopher Demosthenes. Do you know how he became so great? He started by being lousy first. The very first time he gave a speech as a youngster, he fidgeted and stammered badly. Every one laughed at him and suggested that he shouldn't give another public speech ever again. In the following years, Demosthenes set out to change the public's perception of him. He gave his all to improve his diction and vocal power. He spent hours near the ocean practicing vocal variety by putting pebbles on his tongue while he competed with the roar of the ocean. Demosthenes is no longer considered to have been a lousy speaker. He's now often touted as the greatest orator of all time!

What about you? Have you been laughed at when you attempted to sing, write, bake, or dream the impossible? What are you willing to do to change public perception about you? You can, of course, but first you must be willing to be lousy and awkward. You have to not only go through the process, but also you have to enjoy it along the way. Glenna Salsbury and the rest of the people I mentioned earlier did not start as masters. They, over time, became masters. It's not how many times you fail or succeed; it's who you become during the process.

She Wants To Be A Star

"Uncle Rene, I can sing real good. I want to be a star." My niece, Thomasina, said those words to me when she was nine years old. "Why don't you sing a song for me so that I can hear your melodious voice," I told her. "Oh, no," she replied. "I don't want to make a fool out of myself in front of you. I only sing to myself when I am in my room." No!

How in the world can Tommy ever become a star who is able to entertain millions when she doesn't even have the courage to sing in front of her uncle? As you can imagine, she and I had a long conversation about this topic. I shared my philosophy about "Process" with her. I explained to her that many of the people whose pictures she hangs in her room didn't start out as stars. They became stars in the process of spending countless hours working and practicing. Many had been teased and ridiculed. Still, they practiced and rehearsed until they were exhausted while their peers were having fun. They went to bed in the wee hours of the night and woke early to perform and show their talents. They were rejected time and time again until finally they got noticed. They traveled from state to state making appearances in backyard bars and alleys for little or no pay. Real success is not cheap, nor is it easy.

Patrice Douge is one of the best photographers alive, and he has passion for what he does. Patrice is Haitian. For many years, he has given the world community a three dimensional view of Haiti through the lens of his camera. While Patrice's work as a journalist photographer is very well respected around the world, the political situation in Haiti has made it very difficult for him to contribute his talents and skills to his country.

After much thinking, he decided to leave Haiti for New York. What he didn't realize was that he was about to start from scratch again. Patrice suddenly found himself living in the corner of a friend's basement. Depressed and broke, he took a job working forty hours a week. He became even more frustrated. "What I was born to do is photography. That is my life!" Patrice told me. During our conversation, I was able to recharge Patrice's battery. I shared with Patrice many of the same things I am writing about now regarding process. I told Patrice that he was beginning anew. *No Condition is Permanent!* I reminded him. I also shared some specific ideas of ways he can start fresh and live his dreams. I was able to convince him to hang in there and take what had come to his life in stride. Fortunately, it wasn't hard to boost Patrice's confidence because he already had a good plan to start over and succeed in America.

What Kind of Success Do You Want?

In my opinion, there are two kinds of people who pursue success: those who are fascinated by people at the top, and those who are interested in the process taken by people at the top. People from the first group focus all their energy admiring their idol's house, jewelry, cars, fame, and fortune. They will always be chasing the objects of success, which are always fleeting. The other group respects their idol's status; however, they are mostly interested in learning what steps the person took to reach the top—the process. They are interested in the process. This second group studies success instead of worshiping it. Members of this group want to retrace the steps their idol took, and apply all lessons learned. They will truly become successful, and their success will be built on solid ground.

To which group do you belong? The former? I hope the latter. If so, one day you will be at the top rubbing shoulders with the very people who inspired you to be there. However, this won't happen until you first endure and overcome the bottom. You must *earn* your right to be at the top. You have to learn to enjoy the journey.

Exercise

Write down everything you hate doing in your line of work. Now, try to look at each of these things with fresh eyes—eyes that now see the things you hate as necessary steps during your process to success.

Example:

- How might having a boss who overloads you with work teach you lessons that you can apply both personally and professionally?

- How might having your accomplishments overlooked inspire you to acknowledge the accomplishments of others, no matter how small?

- What obstacles do you now have that you can use to your advantage? How do you plan to do that?

Write down your thoughts and emotions. Be practical and specific.

One Last Word

Many of my acquaintances say I was born with special gifts, gifts that helped me become so good in front of an audience. Maybe they are right, but they, too, are gifted. I'm not special. Nature plays no favoritism. If they had seen how nervous and lousy I was during my early days as a speaker, they would reconsider their statement. Still others want to know my secret to success. If you've hung in there this far, I think you now know what those secrets are— starting where I was, enjoying the process, and working hard no matter what.

I'm still continuing my journey. I still have a long way to go. I am still learning. I am still sacrificing time and energy. Success is not a matter of luck, gift, or talent; it's the deliberate and consistent effort of preparation. I hope I was able to persuade my niece that the process requires a great deal of sacrifice. Reaching the top is never easy, nor will it ever be. Any airplane wishing to soar into the skies must first use a lot of fuel and energy getting down the runway.

Waiting is difficult, but the rewards can be phenomenal. The law of delayed gratification says the more time you put into something, the bigger the potential rewards are. The people at the bottom of the ladder usually have a short-term perspective. They want success now. People at the top of the ladder, on the other hand, have a long-term perspective. They project ten, fifteen, and twenty years into the future.

When I first joined the Georgia Speakers Association my friend, Mark Mayberry, told me it would take me five solid years in the business before I could make a living at it. I thought his statement was ridiculous, but Mark was right. The speaking business is hard. It takes a lot of time and energy to establish credibility before folks will trust you enough to put you in front of their audience. That goes for any other type of business as well. It takes a good, solid five years or more of hard work and dedication to get established. Those who succeed are not necessarily the best at what they do. Rather, they are those who hang in there no matter what. They enjoy the process!

CHAPTER FOUR

Stop The Excuses, Please

Stop The Excuses, Please

"Keep away from people who try to belittle your ambitions. Small people always do that, but the really great make you feel that you, too, can become great."— Mark Twain

"Cock-a-doodle-do" the roosters crowed. It's five o'clock in the morning, still dark outside. The street peddlers talk loudly as they make their way to the four corners of the dirt road in Carrefour Joute (the local flea market) to set up shop. Some carry coconuts, mangos, and avocados; others have homemade hats, straw sacks, and other articles. Boys and girls get out of bed and hurry to a wellspring to collect drinking water. They bathe along the river's edge on the way back. Then they start their journey to school. It's Wednesday.

I wake full of excitement. I carry the dirty rags (from the dirt floor on which I slept) to the river to wash them. This time it doesn't matter to me that people tease me; it doesn't matter that the children hold their noses to let me know that my ragged clothes smell of urine. They are only going to school. I, however, am preparing to discover my fate.

At two o'clock in the afternoon, the old, loud truck, Voici Phane *(vwah-see fahn)*, finally arrives. It's coated with mud and dust. The trip from Port-au-Prince to the village has been a trip from hell and the driver is very tired. He stops by Mrs. Adrienne's place to take a quick nap. The porter who loads and unloads the truck tells me something that I had already learned from a neighbor the day before—my mother has finally sent for me. At first I doubted that the neighbor had told me the truth. Now I know I can believe him, so I dance a happy little dance of joy and liberation. No more breadfruit for breakfast, lunch, and dinner. It bloats my stomach and makes me sick.

I run down to the ocean one last time and splash in the water. "Thank you, God!" I shout over the ocean's waves. "I am finally leaving this awful village. Too many people poke fun at me. I feel weak and miserable!" The huge and ugly pig that scares me so much has followed me, as if it knows I am about to leave. You know, I used to threaten to kill that pig if it didn't stay away from me; but Betila, the lady with whom I was staying, would not have appreciated it. The pig was all her fortune. Besides, there was no strength in my weak body to wrestle any pig.

At seven years old, I am about to meet the woman who had mustered all of her courage to walk away from her nine-month-old baby boy. I'm also about to meet my sister, Andrele, and my brother, Roberto. Word has gotten out about my trip to Port-Au-Prince, so folks in the village come to bid me goodbye. For the first time, I feel like I am noticed! I feel like I am visible!

The Trip Was Long And Tiresome

We were packed in the truck like sardines. There was no room to move—barely room to breathe. We literally had to stop often to repair the road or to push Voici Phane. It took us two full days to travel a distance that would have taken us only two hours on smoother highways. Port-Au-Prince was overwhelming: concrete pavement, tall buildings, and lights illuminating every street and corridor. Since I had grown up in a village in the backwoods of the Island, I had imagined that the city would be quieter. How wrong I was!

My sister and brother, Andrele and Roberto, were waiting for me on the curb. I hugged them. Maman was out working hard in order to buy us food for the day. When she arrived, she dropped the brown bag that contained our meal and enthusiastically held me in her arms. My swollen tummy and skeletal arms and legs spoke loudly to her heart. She had known I was sick, but she didn't know how seriously my condition had deteriorated.

Maman was full of guilt. Before I met my mother on that day, she could not afford the fifty cents to send for me. She was having a tough life in the City, barely surviving. She lived in a little shack with one tiny hole as a window. The shack was infested with rats and roaches, and it was always dark. She did not own much in the way of furniture. At night, Maman slept on a dilapidated iron bed, which squeaked all night. My sister, my brother, and I slept on ragged sheets tossed on the floor. There were mornings when I woke to rats nibbling the bottom of my feet. Today, I wonder how we ever overcame that kind of life!

It's Up To You

Do you remember what I said to you about the need to tell your story? Well, this is my story. Today, people have a hard time imagining my having had that kind of life; but that's the way it was. The reason I can share my story with you today is that I believed that somehow, some way, life was going to get better. I also knew it would require every ounce of energy I had. I had to work very hard.

One thing I didn't do at the time was to blame anyone else for my childhood. One of the most destructive habits people have is playing the blaming game. As a society, we are always looking for ways to shift the blame away from ourselves onto others. We learn this as children, and the idea continues throughout our adult lives. In America, one can get away with many things. Every day I see grown men and women crying and pointing their fingers at others on television. The rapist says he was abused as a child. The man beats his wife because he had an abusive parent. The criminal kills because he was temporarily insane. Someone fails to get a good education because he or she grew up in the ghetto. The list goes on.

Part of this may be true; I don't intend to discount the research done by psychologists. However, in my opinion, blaming others becomes a self-fulfilling prophecy. I simply want people to wake up and take full responsibility for their lives. Don't blame others—make better choices instead! I wonder where I would be today if I had wasted my energy blaming others for the way my life was in Haiti.

Now some might take this the wrong way and mistakenly call me insensitive. That's okay. My goal is to give you reasons why *you* should start living *your* dreams. I want you to get up and go *now*! I am not in the business of handing out excuses. It would go against my entire belief system. I am sensitive. I do care. That's why I am asking you not to waste any more time. Today you can do just a little to prevent your future from looking like your past. Every day offers you fresh opportunities to prepare yourself for a better tomorrow. Resolve to look ahead. START NOW!

When I look at my life—where I came from, the kind of environment in which I grew up—I should never have been able to become a writer, speaker, or consultant. The odds were stacked against me. I could easily have used a mountain of excuses. Yet, I know that the mind works mysteriously; and whatever I believe becomes my reality. Within the first year after I had arrived in America, I saw a country where opportunities abounded. To me, the American Dream was everywhere. On the other hand, many who are born in the U.S. spend their entire lives building a case to explain why they can't make it. The difference is in our perspective—in our priorities.

Yes, it is extremely hard for certain people to make it in this country. It was certainly difficult for me. I didn't speak English, and my education was very limited. Every time I opened my mouth, people automatically assumed I wasn't intelligent. Yet, I had the audacity to believe that I could become a success in spite of my challenges.

What about you? Do you believe you can succeed? What barriers do you have to overcome? Do you have to learn how to speak English? One man told me that, because I am an immigrant, I receive all kinds of help not available to others. Excuse me! I have never received a penny from the U.S. government! I have never even collected unemployment. When I couldn't get a job because of my inability to speak English, I started washing cars on the streets of Miami for five dollars each. Then I became a boat carpenter. In fact, I worked very hard at many odd jobs while I was learning to speak English. However, I had more to learn than to only speak English. I had to learn to read. I had to educate myself.

Once I began to acquire more knowledge, I experienced a dramatic shift in the quality of my life. I was able to get better jobs. I continued to saturate my brain with more of the knowledge that I had gleaned from books. As the old cliché goes: "The more you know the more you grow; the more you learn, the more you earn." It may be an old cliché all right, but it is certainly true for me! What about you? Is it time for you to upgrade your skills?

It is really up to you! If I can do it, so can you. I believed, and I gave it my best shot. Once you believe wholeheartedly that you can do the thing you want to do, you've got to give all you've got. The world is nothing but ideas. Everything you see was first an idea. Yet, an idea that only resides in the mind is like an automobile without fuel. You must take action. Your energy, belief, and passion fuel the idea. No one can provide that kind of fuel for you. It's up to you!!

Only Your Best Will Do

"If a man can write a better book, preach a better sermon, or make a better mouse-trap than his neighbor, though he builds his house in the woods, the world will make a beaten path to his door."—Ralph Waldo Emerson

Maman didn't make excuses for herself either. Yes, she was sick! Yes, she was broke! Yes, she was depressed! She lived from hand to mouth. Her tomorrows were very unpredictable. She might as well have been working as a slave because she never came home with a check. She had to pay her creditors.

With three children to raise and three dollars ($3.00) a month to pay in rent, Maman barely earned enough to feed the family. I can remember when she didn't have money at Christmastime to buy us gifts. It was painful for her to see other kids flashing their toys in our face. Maman did not have a logical explanation why life was the way it was, but she always encouraged us—particularly me—to strive for the best. She always told us, "I don't want you to grow up having it as tough as I have. Get an education. It is your passport out of poverty. And always do your best." She always prayed that we would grow up and make her proud.

Turn Negatives Into Positives

After I joined my mother in the city, I no longer worried about my father. It had become clear to me that I was fatherless. It didn't bother me as much as people thought it did. I must admit, however, that every time my sister and brother's father came for a visit, the thought of not having a father of my own crossed my mind. Fortunately, their father was very considerate. Whenever he gave something to my brother and sister, he would always give me equal share.

All along I knew that if something happened to my mother, I would have to provide for myself. Being fatherless did not bother me as much as it motivated me. I continued to predict a promising future for myself. I became extremely curious. I always looked for ways to improve my life. I refused to be average. I gave nothing but my very best every time, and that's what Maman expected from me, too.

Can you honestly say that you are giving your best every time? Are you ordinary or extraordinary? If you are not giving your best at whatever you are doing, you are cheating somebody; and that somebody is you. If you want to go from making a living to becoming wealthy, you must go from being average to being excellent. When you find yourself facing a disadvantage, such as being fatherless or being a foreigner who is unable to speak the natives' language, you have to do more than is expected of you. Any time there is a negative in your life, you have to find the positive in you and combine it with the problem to create power. GIVE YOUR BEST! Find creative ways to improve upon what you are now doing each and every time you do it. You do that and the world will be ready to shower you with money and admiration.

She Can Fix A Mean Gumbo

My friend, Connie Payton, a talented writer and speaker, is from New Orleans. She can fix a mean gumbo. The smell alone will make you drool. Connie once explained to me what it takes to pre-pare gumbo. It's a long process. She said to me that few people enjoy being there to see the mess. However, people love to eat her gumbo. Have you ever had a party where your friends and family members eat and drink and then leave you to deal with the mess?

It's the same with life. When you succeed, there are hosts of people who will call you 'friend.' They will use your name to impress others. They will want to help you when you don't need the help. (Banks are this way. When you need money, they refuse to give you a loan; but once you become successful, they beat a path to your door to lend you money.) Some of your friends will want to sit at the table with you to enjoy your gumbo, but they have no idea what you went through to cook it. They missed the mess altogether.

When my speaking business began, I was the accountant, the marketing director, the sales person, and the secretary. I took out the trash, too! If you are a small business owner, and a one-man operation, you know what I am talking about. I had to juggle between a full-time job and my business. I would come home after a networking function with great leads, but with no time to call or drop anyone a note. I really needed some help, but I couldn't afford to pay anybody. I tried enlisting the help of others, to no avail. They couldn't see my dream. Some were too busy; others simply didn't care. In other words, I often had to cook my own gumbo and deal with the mess myself. Many times I couldn't rely on anyone to assist me as I began my journey to success. I had to find my own inspiration to get me going.

Inspiration Vs. Motivation

When I mention to others that I am a motivational speaker, the most common reply is, "Motivate me." My response usually is, "Today's my day off." I joke about it because contrary to what most people think, we should not aim for motivation. Rather, we should aim for inspiration. Most of my motivational speaker friends would agree with me that motivation is nothing but a fleeting experience. It is like a caffeine boost. It only lasts for a moment. I am sure my words motivate others. I have heard that many times, but my ultimate goal is to provide lasting inspiration to my audiences. I believe that once you are inspired, lasting motivation will follow. You see, lasting motivation comes from within; it's the internal flame that sets you afire. If you can't wake up in the morning and pep yourself up, you are in big trouble. The best way to remain internally motivated is to look for sources of inspiration. I will tell you how to do that later.

On the other hand, there is external motivation. External motivation is a lot like taking drugs. You can easily become addicted, and whatever motivates you had better be there all the time. Once the person or thing that motivated you is no longer present, you go right back to where you started. It's a short-term feeling. Here is a classic example: I had a boss who was power hungry. He wanted to rule with an iron fist. I am sure he had good intentions. He wanted to shine, but he used the wrong approach to motivate us. We did what he wanted us to do, but only when he was around. Had my boss possessed the gift of leadership, he would have found a way to inspire us. Once inspired, we would be motivated to do an excellent job and to make him shine even when no one was watching. (By the way, if you are in a leadership position, here is how you can inspire others: create heartwarming stories. Do something extraordinary for a couple of employees at the bottom. You will create inspirational stories that last forever.)

A second example comes to mind. Suppose you went to a multilevel marketing meeting. Right after the meeting you got very excited and pumped up. You signed up on the spot. However, unless you were truly inspired, two days later, you ended up with a nice kit and no desire to go into the business. Does that mean multilevel marketing was a gimmick? No. It means you were motivated, not inspired. In fact, multilevel marketing is one of the best, low-cost and no-cost ways to become a millionaire in America. But you have to give it all you've got. You have to be inspired and refuse to let negative people rain on your parade.

Let's face it, inspiration can last a lifetime. Do you remember a time when you were inspired either by a teacher, a friend, or a parent? Was it a movie, an autobiography, or a warm story? Years later, you are still inspired by that event. Right? I believe that once you are inspired, you will find the wherewithal to move and take action.

The next time you find yourself caught up in the moment, ask yourself whether you are inspired or motivated. There is a huge difference between the two. If you are waiting for external motivation to get you going day in and day out, you will always live a life of disappointment. If you are going to start something phenomenal, find the inspiration to wake up in the morning fired up and ready to go.

Here is how you can do it:

1. Read autobiographies of people who have accomplished amazing things in spite of overwhelming odds.

2. Listen to exciting speeches and sermons.

3. Draw upon the amazing stories of your parents, friends, and acquaintances. Let them inspire you.

4. Finally, draw upon the stories of successful people who have proven they can brave the storms. Ask them to share their stories with you. They'd love to do so if asked; and you will demonstrate to them that you are interested in the process—in what made them successful.

No Condition Is Permanent! *by Rene Godefroy*

It boils down to this: you've got to believe! When you are inspired by a story, there is something on the inside of you that causes you to believe. It's like having a little voice inside your head saying, "If Rene can do it in spite of the challenges he has faced, I believe I can too." Do you see my point? Somewhere, deep down inside, people who are inspired tend to have a stronger belief system in spite of the doubters around them. The next time you realize that there is no fire inside your belly to ignite your passion, look for inspiration. Read autobiographies. Listen to great speeches and sermons. Ask successful people who have had great comebacks to share their stories with you, or to even mentor you. One day, your story will be inspiring, too!

CHAPTER FIVE

Look For The Stars
In Your Darkest Moment

Look For The Stars
In Your Darkest Moment

"The pain you feel is the breaking of the shell that encloses your understanding."—Khalil Gibran

I greeted great-grandma Stephane. "Good morning Grandma. How are you today?" She gave me a panged expression. "Good morning, son", she said. "Oh, my body is giving up on me." She then pulled her hand out from under her pillow and handed me half of her bread—her breakfast. That was our morning routine. No matter how small the piece of bread, Great-grandma Stephane would always save me half. She was in her late eighty's, and she was not well. Still I would come to her. Why? She made me feel safe. She made me feel better, too. My stomach was tense and bloated with parasites; and when Great-grandma tapped on it, it sounded like a drum. However, she made me drink kerosene from the night lamp to help ease my constant indigestion (she was a roots doctor and a midwife). It may seem incredible to you, but her medicine was always a relief for me!

"Good morning, Grandma." I said one morning. She didn't respond. Since she was so old, I thought that she was losing her hearing. I moved closer to her wooden bed and said, "Great-grandma, I just said good morning. You didn't hear me, did you?" She still didn't say anything. Betila, the lady with whom I was staying, came from behind and broke the news. "Great-grandma died in the middle of the night." My short and caring relationship with Great-grandma Stephane was over.

As you might imagine, I was devastated. I thought that life was unfair. Now that Great-grandma was gone, no one would comfort me in my moments of deep sorrow and uncertainty, or remind me that soon my mother would come for me. I had to face my dark moments alone. Great-grandma was gone. No one would be there to hold my hand or make me feel safe. I'd no longer receive compassion from her caring eyes.

Have you ever known someone who made you feel safe and secure during trials and tribulations? If so, have you suddenly had that person vanish? What can you do? You must carry on. *That* is the best way to honor that person. When you give up and abandon hope, you defeat the whole purpose of life. I celebrate Great-grandma Stephane every time I give an outstanding speech and my listeners leap to their feet in standing ovation—every time I successfully achieve something significant. Becoming everything you are capable of is the highest respect you can pay to the people who nurture or who have nurtured your soul.

Focus On Your Stars; Not Your Darkness

Nights were very dark in my village. It was not like you could fumble around your house or apartment looking for a light switch. There were no lights, period. No streetlights or office lights illuminated the pathways. On most nights, I had to hurry home before nightfall, or I would be caught outside in the dark, tripping in potholes, fumbling barefoot with the soles of my feet exposed to thorns, cacti, sharp rocks, and other dangers. I know you weren't born in a tiny village without electricity, but I am sure you have faced challenges similar to those I faced in the village. There are times when your world is so dark you stumble and you can't even see your path. Just like it was for me, your pathways can get so treacherous that your feet slide on the mud and you fall flat on you back.

On top of all that, the old myths of my village would run through my head—stories about spirits of the departed ones lurking in the dark, waiting to scare people. They called these spirits zombies—those who died because someone put a spell on them. Rumors and gossip were what made me so afraid. I believed the lies! Zombies weren't real. I am sure you can remember moments in your life when you, too, were uncertain and afraid of something that never actually happened. Perhaps you wanted to undertake something, but you were too paralyzed with fear to do so. Perhaps you're paralyzed with fear this very moment. Well, stop believing the lies. Your zombies aren't real either!

In my tiny village, life seemed like a long, dark and narrow pathway with no end in sight. I'll never forget one particular night when, as a little boy, I sat alone in utter darkness and gazed into the skies. The stars began to reveal themselves. I was fascinated because while it was dark on the ground, the sky became bright and shiny. I also discovered that the stars appeared to shine most brightly on the darkest nights. Something about them brightened my inner world. Something about them gave me hope. The more I focused on those stars, the more I became oblivious of my agonies. I was no longer afraid of zombies. In that moment, I gained the courage and strength to stay in the race. I went from despair to hope.

The stars assured me that my condition wasn't permanent. Today, I look for those stars in a different form; and that makes a tremendous difference in my life. It can for you, too. I also learned to pray, trust, and be patient. I have also found that a sunny day always follows the dark night. Are you going through some challenges in your life now that you wish would go away? Are you in a dark place in your life? Have you abandoned hope in ever reaching your heart's desires? If you are surrounded by darkness—divorce, sickness, death, or layoff—you need to be patient and trust that the sun with burst through your darkness. Don't give up. There are stars in your skies, too! No Condition is Permanent! It shall pass.

Look And You Shall See Them

You know what I mean! There are circumstances over which you have no control that come your way and rock your world. Those are the times when your stars shine most brightly. You have a choice to make. You can focus on the darkness—or the stars.

You may ask, "Man, what stars are you talking about? Where are they?" These stars are everywhere; they are glittering somewhere in the valley of your darkness. Do you have a child who brings a smile to your face after a long and stressful day at work? What about all the people who have passed through your life? Can their stories of triumph be a star to light your pathway or inspire you? What about the thousand things you can be grateful for in spite of your problems and disappointments? Do you count the gifts and talents God has given you? Do you count your blessings? Come on! You know what I mean. Those are your stars—your hope. The darker your life is, the brighter those stars shine. In fact, the darkness allows your stars to be revealed to you. They are your lessons, your wisdom, and your insights.

I know it's hard to sometimes believe that life can treat you so badly. However, how would you ever see the stars if there were no darkness? How can you ever grow and learn without challenges? You might say, "That's easy to say. You just don't know my situation." As my friend Marcia Steele often says, "I am with you." I understand what you mean, but you can't grow without traversing dark moments in your journey. I wish I had better news for you. Sometimes being positive requires us to accept the things we can't change or control. Know what they are and move on anyway.

Mitchell Is The Man

W. Mitchell, the author of *It's Not What Happens To You, It's What You Do About It*, is the man who cemented my belief about focusing on the stars. More than twenty years ago, Mitchell had a terrible motorcycle accident. A truck ran into him. The gas tank of his motorcycle popped and spilled gas over him; the friction ignited the fuel. Mitchell became a human torch. He was burnt from head to toe. That accident left him completely disfigured. The doctors had to cut his toes to attach to his hands. Mitchell had a decision to make. He could give up and live in misery for the rest of his life, or he could focus on his stars.

It wasn't an easy decision. Many people were embarrassed looking at his disfigured face. Children ran away from him yelling, "Monster! Monster!" Yet Mitchell chose to focus on his stars. He went on to become one of the most respected personalities in the country. He has built a huge company. One evening, Mitchell cranked up his airplane. As soon as he took off, the plane crashed. He woke up after months in a coma to find himself in a wheelchair, a tool he would need for the rest of his life. You might be thinking, "That's it for Mitchell." No!

Today, Mitchell is a highly successful businessman, author, and speaker. I first heard Mitchell's story from his good friend, Anthony Robbins. I was inspired. The day I gave my keynote speech to more than two thousand professional speakers for the National Speakers Association in Washington, D.C., I met the man himself. I thought, "Mitchell, you are the man." He rolled his wheelchair close to me, looked at me with a penetrating stare, and said, "You were awesome! Every one needs to hear your message." Wow! What an incredible privilege to receive the blessings of such an outstanding human being.

Mitchell's entire philosophy about life is simple: "It's not what happens to you; it's what you do about it." He says that he could do 10,000 things before the accident. Now he can only do 9,000. He says that he dwells on the 9,000—his stars—and that makes all the difference for him. Wow!

What about you? At this stage in your life, what really matters to you? What do you focus on? Mitchell looked through his darkness and saw the stars. Today, he is a world-renowned motivational speaker touching the lives of millions. He didn't focus on the dark; he continued to seek out its stars.

Mitchell has given me encouragement and heartfelt advice since I met him. He has opened some doors for me by referring me to some of his clients. When my future in the speaking business looks dark, Mitchell helps me see the stars. When you have people around you who can light up your path in the dark, they are your stars. I am so grateful I crossed Mitchell's path on my journey. Just remember, you don't have to hit the stage at the National Speakers Association to find the Mitchells of the world. Look up; look everywhere. You will see them. They are your past successes, perhaps your friends or family members, or even total strangers.

Your Gifts Are In Your Problems

I once heard a minister say that when God sends you a gift, he wraps it up in a problem. The bigger the problem is, the bigger the gift. I agree. Don't you? I know this is difficult to accept. I wonder how many times I missed receiving a gift from God because I cursed the problem. Do you feel that way sometimes? Do you ever say, "God, why me?" I have said that on many occasions, but you know what? That didn't change things or make the situation better. It's like going through a violent storm. You don't have any control over the storm other than to wait and trust that it will pass; and yes, if you really trust and believe, the storm will pass.

Whether you agree with me or not, there is a gift, a lesson buried inside every problem. Think about it; everything that you and I are enjoying today was first someone else's problem. Then, that person created an invention to solve the problem. Therefore, the problem arrived with the solution bundled inside. Simple logic, isn't it?

Unfortunately, many people spend their lives running away from problems. I understand this. When we are mired in darkness and misery, it's difficult to stop and look for the gifts. We become like a deer in the headlights; we're focused solely on the dark. Are you familiar with Murphy's Law? It says that whatever can go wrong will go wrong, and at the worst possible time. No wonder so many of us experience Murphy's Law. Whatever we constantly dwell upon tends to grow. In other words, we receive more of it. That is not the way of high achievers.

Stop Worrying About The Wrong Things

You and I spend a great amount of our time and energy worrying about things. Quite frankly, I don't know if anyone can claim that he or she never worries. Now listen to this: Worry can wear you out. Years ago I read an article about fog. I found out that fog is nothing but water. An entire neighborhood covered with fog has the equivalent of only one cup of water. However, that cup of water can make driving very dangerous for commuters. The same is true about worry; it only takes a little to deeply affect you.

What do you worry about? Let's remember the fog. If I threw a tiny, insignificant drop of water on you, would that make you depressed? No, of course not. All right, could it be that what is pressing you down at the moment may be nothing but fog? Don't you see? Most of our unhappiness is nothing but a tiny drop of water…one that evaporates to create a huge fog over us.

According to most studies about what people worry about, it's believed that 90 percent of our worries never come to pass. In most cases, these worries are things we can't control or change anyway. There's more. The same studies tell us that six percent of the things we worry about are mindless criticisms from others; three percent are so trivial we should have never even thought about them in the first place. I don't know about you, but I can personally identify with those findings. According to those same findings, only one percent of your worries have any basis as actual concerns in your life. My question to you is this: Can you tell what comprises that one-percent in your life? Tough question isn't it?

Here is my rule of thumb: If you can't change or control something, you need to find a way to let it go. The Serenity prayer (as adapted by Alcoholics Anonymous) echoes this: *"God, grant me the serenity to accept the things I cannot change, the courage to change the things I can, and the wisdom to know the difference."* What about you? When worries are pressing you down, what do you say? Isn't this a marvelous short prayer to memorize? I think so.

Through It All You Will Get Stronger

*"Circumstance does not make the man; it reveals
him to himself."*—James Allen, *As A Man Thinketh*

Friedrich Nietzsche said it best: "What does not kill you will make
you stronger." The furniture makers in my village venture great
distances to find mighty trees. Since ancient time, furniture makers have had the unwavering belief that the trees that survive
adverse weather conditions—sun, storms, and rain—are strong
and more resistant to pressure. The quality of the furniture, they
believe, is directly related to how many years and how many
blows the tree endured from Mother Nature.

How many blows have you received from Mother Nature lately? Many? Then the next question is: What have you learned from
those blows that you can consistently apply to your life to achieve
better results? Take a look at the top people in your field or profession. The two percent of those people at the top are those who have
withstood the test of time. They took one blow after another, yet
they continued to learn and make adjustments. They have Bull Dog
tenacity. That is where the differences in the size of their paychecks
come from. When we believe, learn from our challenges, and apply
the lessons to better our tomorrow, our value to society goes up.

Bumpy, Hilly, And Dusty

In July 2001, I took a trip to my village. I rode in the rear of a truck
from the city to the village. I had forgotten how tough the roads
were. Man, I was bouncing the whole way! The roads were
bumpy, hilly, and dusty. Then I returned to Atlanta, Georgia, near
where I live. Cruising the flat and smooth highways was a big contrast. After visiting my village, I enjoyed and appreciated the roads
around Atlanta a lot more than before. It's all about having a contrast—something with which to compare things.

The rough moments on our journey prepare us to enjoy and
appreciate the smooth ones. They are our teachers. The Zen
philosopher Lao Tzu says, "When the student is ready, the teacher

---

appears." The same challenge you are confronting can be your teacher. Perhaps the person who makes your life bumpy or who makes you sick is your teacher. Learn from him or her and move on. Maybe that person is creating contrast in your life. Do you see where I am coming from? You and I can change our outer world by changing our inner world—the way we view our circumstances.

There Is One Problem-Free Place On Earth

A young American student had recently acquired his PhD in philosophy after many long years of study. He was particularly interested in eastern philosophy. After graduation, he went to India to study with a spiritual guru. When he got there, the first question he asked the master was how he could live a life without problems. The master was taken aback by the young lad's question, but he promised to show his young student such a place.

The master blindfolded the student's eyes and led him to a place where problems don't exist. When they got there, the spiritual guru said to the young man, "This is the place you inquired about. You can live here all your life without any problems." The young man said, "But I am blindfolded, sir. I can't see. Is it a beautiful place?" "Yes," replied the guru, "It is adorned with colorful flowers. Can't you smell them?" The young man said, "Of course I can. This is my ideal place." The spiritual guru took the blindfold off the young man's eyes. Low and behold, the young man found himself standing in the middle of a cemetery. The guru said, "Young man, you have a choice; you can live here with no problems or you can face the world."

It isn't the size of our problems that brings us down; it's the size of our courage. I am not suggesting, by any means, that you should be merry and ignore your problems because they will eventually go away. I am only encouraging you to look up in the skies and see the stars, to be patient and stay as positive as you can. The church folks sing a song that says, *Sometimes, Lord, I wonder how I got over.* One day you will be able to say the same thing, too. Since we've established that I can't solve your problems, I am going to share with you some tips on how to brave your storms.

7 Ways To Deal With Problems And Stress

1) Don't Just Sit There. Move!

According to many psychologists, motion creates emotion. You might notice that when you are idle, it's easier to become depressed. Your heart rate slows down, less oxygen travels to your brain, and you are slumped somewhere in a chair blocking air from reaching your lungs. I challenge you right now, regardless of how you are feeling, to get up and start jumping up and down. Try it now for a minute. Back already? Well, how do you feel? Be honest—don't you feel better? Ah, it works like magic. (Shame on you for not doing what I asked you to do.) Movement is a wonderful solution to stress and depression. Do you know why we tend to get depressed more at night while we are relaxing? It's because we aren't moving. From now on, write the word MOVE in big, bold letters and place it where you can see this word frequently. When you feel a little down, go to the gym for a workout or go to the park for a walk or run. Remember this: everything in life is in perpetual motion. When water does not move and flow, it becomes unhealthy. When blood is not circulating, it clogs up and makes us sick. It's the same for you and me. Where there is no movement, there is depression and slow death. Move! Do something!

2) Smell The Roses

Like my friend Jan Toles says, "Go smell the roses." (Jan, I listened to your advice and went to the flower section in Kroger and literally smelled every rose. That's what you get for not being clear to foreigners!) How do you smell the roses? How about investing some money to go on that one trip you've been dreaming about? Would Paris do? There you will find lots of exotic places to jolt your imagination and spur your creativity. You can also visit the Caribbean and learn how to scuba dive. Can you imagine swimming deep under the beautiful blue water alongside some of the most beautiful creatures you have ever seen? When my friend Lumenise Gilot described that experience to me, I thought to myself, "What an exceptional way to smell the roses!"

If Paris or the Caribbean is too farfetched for you, just stay home. The reality is that you don't even have to travel to faraway places to smell the roses. Sit in your backyard or in a nearby park and enjoy the cheerful melody of birds singing all around. Go to an amusement park with a child or toss Frisbees in the city park nearby. Take a trip to that little historical town in your area where I am sure you will discover the same creative genius that makes Paris such a beautiful city. While there, take the time to marvel at the incredible human creations. All you need to do is to observe. Visit some antique shops. You might say, "Well, I am not into antiques." I am not into antiques either. However, anytime I visit one of those shops, I find myself transported in a time I have never seen before. I often visualize the creator of a certain piece dedicating countless hours to creating something that will outlast him or her.

3) Get Some Company
If you're like me, you have many acquaintances, but you only have a few true friends. This isn't because I'm introverted. It is because I'm very selective about who I let enter my territory. I have worked too hard to build my house—my dream—and I won't let anyone destroy it for me in the blink of an eye. When you're feeling down, call your true friends and share what it is that you're going through. Ask for their advice or input. While their advice or suggestions may be helpful, often you'll find that simply verbalizing your problems will help you feel better.

4) Help Others Cope With Their Problems
It is very therapeutic when you engross yourself in helping others. You will be surprised how many people's problems are worse than those you may be facing. You can offer others assistance in countless ways. Don't curl up in your bed and let depression and stress take hold of you. Get out and help somebody. There are many charitable organizations that can use your help right now. My dear cousin Barbara reads to the blind. What about that? Call the National Federation of the Blind so that they can tell you how to get involved.

5) Laugh A Little

By now you've heard that laughter is a good internal medicine. It relieves tension and loosens the muscles. It causes blood to flow to the heart and brain. More importantly, laughter releases a chemical that rids the body of pains. Yet, this is just the tip of the iceberg. Every day, researchers discover new benefits of laughter. Let me ask you this question: "Can you use a good dose of belly shaking laughter every now and then?" Of course you can. Here's what you can do:

a. Go to comedy clubs as often as you can afford.

b. Watch funny movies.

c. Write down all your embarrassing moments. They were embarrassing when you experienced them. Now, they are your funnies. Share them with your friends. They will laugh with you.

d. Record everything you observe that makes you laugh and share it with your friends.

e. Do what my friend and editor extraordinaire, Pat Toles, does. Browse the "humorous" section of greeting card shops and purchase the cards that make you laugh. You'll have them to experience over and over again or to share with a friend.

6) Visit Third World Countries

Nothing is more humbling than to visit a poor country and see first hand what other human beings go through just to survive. Most people who have taken such trips come back with a deep and profound sense of gratitude and appreciation. They realize how much they've taken for granted without ever realizing it. I encourage you to travel whenever you can afford to do so. You're not too busy. Do it for you. Your life will never be the same.

7) Wear Your Knees Out

If there were one sustainable remedy I could offer you when the going gets tough, it would be prayer. Many people, depending on their faith, might call it meditation. It doesn't matter to me what you call it, as long as you have a place to run to. Mahatma Gandhi said, "Religions are crossroads converging upon the point." Well, I don't often discuss religion, and I don't know what works for you; but Christianity is the way I know. However, I am sensitive enough to respect your faith. My whole point is that when everything else fails, prayer works!

He Felt Devastated And Unworthy. Then He Prayed

A man was trying his hands at several businesses without any success. Every time he opened a business, he failed. His partners always betrayed him. He felt devastated and unworthy. He eventually filed for bankruptcy, but he continued to pray faithfully for guidance. One day, out of exasperation, he decided to start one last business. He revisited his original passion. He was an awesome clothes maker.

This time, the man who had failed so many times before refused to bring any partner to his clothing business. Out of desperation, he threw himself on the floor and prayed. He said, "Lord I am tired of failing. I am tired of being embarrassed in front of my family and friends. I don't want to be betrayed anymore. I need your help. I am starting a business and I want to go where my heart is—where my passion is. Lord, I am going in business with you. I want you to be my partner, and I want to put you first." Today, one of the greatest and best clothing stores in America is Lord & Taylor.

Do you pray when your pathway is dark and cluttered with obstacles? I read this story about Lord & Taylor from a book. I don't have a research team to confirm its authenticity, but it sure makes lots of sense to me. Prayer is terrific medicine.

No Condition Is Permanent! *by Rene Godefroy*

Sitting on the ocean's edge was this little house where I once lived and barely survived. It was completely wiped out by Hurricane Hugo in 1989.

This is Uncle Francois. During one of my return visits home, he took me to the place on top of the hills where great-grandparents once lived.

Aunt Zette and I are in her kitchen holding a fresh stem of green plantain.

There is a lot of breadfruit in the village. They are extremely starchy. Some people boil and eat them. Others beat them to a pulp and swallow small chunks with gumbo sauce—a dish known as toomtoom.

This is the little kitchen where I used to warm up the leftover breadfruit that I often ate. Breadfruit was hard to digest so it was painful to have to eat it.

During the latter part of his life, Uncle Minnes asked me to replace the straw roof over his hut with a tin one. Tin roofs are a sign of progress to many in the village. I am sorry I could not afford to grant his wish before he passed away.

Zo, a guy I knew from the village, came by to see me. He brought fresh coconuts.

CHAPTER SIX

See With Fresh Eyes

See With Fresh Eyes

---

*"The greatest joy of a thinking man is to have searched
the explored and to quietly revere the unexplored."*
—Johann Wolfgang von Goethe

"You idiot! When it was time to satisfy your bestial, sexual appetite, you took the liberty to abuse this poor, innocent woman. You used your power and money to entice her. Then you found it beneath your dignity to associate yourself with her or with me. You refused to claim me as your child. Yet, today you are so proud of my accomplishments and you are going around saying, 'this is my son.' What audacity! God will deal with you accordingly!"

Those were the words of my script in the play *L'enfant Bâtard*—The Fatherless Child. It was 1981, and I performed theatre with a small Haitian group in a little Catholic Church. We rented a large room to perform. On the day of the performance, only 30 people showed up out of the 300 we expected. All the performers were discouraged...except me. I enjoyed my role in the play—that of a fatherless child chastising a man for his lack of responsibility. What's more, I played the part well; I gave it passion and conviction. I didn't have an education in theater. In fact, to this day, I don't know many of the techniques actors use. My acting and reacting were based on trial and error. I relied on my instincts. I suppose I was good because I was, indeed, a fatherless child.

After the play, a man who owned a theatre company, Mr. Rodriguez, came by to look for me. He said he saw me on stage and that he thought I was fabulous! He invited me to audition for his company. Although he wasn't paying his actors, I accepted the offer. The next day I showed up for rehearsal. I played many insignificant roles before I was trusted with bigger ones.

How To Get Promoted Quick

What role are you playing now? During the short time that I was with the theater company in Haiti, I learned a life-changing lesson, one I want to pass on to you now. I learned that whatever we want to achieve in life, we have to begin first by playing with that future role in mind. I was playing less important roles for Mr. Rodriguez's theatre company, but I had my sights set on bigger ones. I wanted to step to the front as one of the main actors. So, I began to memorize the main actors' scripts. I was proactive. One day during rehearsal, we found out that one of the leading actors dropped out. I was called upon to fill his spot. Why? I was the only one who knew his script!

If you need a promotion where you work, you must first start preparing for the role required in the new position. Yes, you will be doing more than you are paid for; but people usually avoid buying goods or services they have not had an opportunity to sample. Employers are the same way, too. If you are really interested in moving up in the company, you have to be proactive. Initiate and anticipate.

As a speaker, there were many times when I had to speak in front of certain groups for free to showcase my speaking talents. You, too, should sometimes decide to showcase your talents. Showcasing your talent is by far the best way to let the world know about the gifts you have in store. Does everybody you come in contact with know what you can do? One way to let them know is to start acting as if you were already in the position for which you are aiming. Once you demonstrate your ability to play the part, you will be the one selected when promotion time comes. Mr.

Rodriguez couldn't help but promote me as one of the main actors in the play because I had demonstrated my qualifications. Have you demonstrated to the people at the top what you can do lately?

Please note that this requires an investment on your part. Yes, you may have to showcase your talents for free. If you own your own business, for example, you may have to give away your services or goods to potential new customers, particularly when business is slow. However, this isn't wasted money. It's a wise investment in your future.

A Promising Future

While I was with the theatre group, rumor had it that we were to travel to Montreal, Canada, to perform. Mr. Rodriguez later confirmed the rumor. I couldn't believe it! After many years fantasizing about airplanes, I was going to be in one! My dream of coming to America seemed closer than ever, as I had heard that Canada was near the United States. At last, after enduring so many blows from poverty, the moment had arrived for me to follow another long pathway. I was about to do what my mother had done when she left our tiny village to discover the possibilities that life had in store for her in Port-au-Prince. Once I made it out of Haiti, I knew I wasn't coming back!

Yes, I was going to miss some of my friends and the Caribbean sunrises and sunsets, but the future that awaited was too promising for me to worry about those things. Besides, living anywhere else was far better than remaining here and enduring the meanness of the tonton macoute (tahn tahn mah coot)—the oppressive Haitian militia army. I was ready to start on a journey that would eventually transform my life forever. Are you thinking about starting your journey to greater success? Why not now? It may transform your life forever! You will never know if all you do is think about it. Indecision can cause you to live a life of regret. Be excited! Go for it!

You see, the thought of going to Montreal along with the possibility of making my way to America thrilled and excited me. At night I could barely sleep. I equated being in America with automatically becoming rich. I didn't know then that poverty on any level existed in America. I didn't know there were homeless people and rundown neighborhoods. I had seen the American tourists walking with nice clothing and expensive jewelry on the streets of Champs de Mars, the famous park where Haitian kids go on Sunday afternoons to play. The tourists looked different, and they spoke a language that sounded like gibberish to me; but they projected an aura of wealth. In my mind, I said that if all Americans were anything like the ones that I had been meeting, the path to America, regardless how difficult it may be, would certainly be worth taking.

Can you imagine how I felt when I found out I was leaving Haiti? Have you ever had something big happen in your life that you knew was a major turning point? When was the last time you had a new beginning? The day I left Haiti was my biggest turning point—it was an ending, but also a new beginning. I knew I had a long way to go, but at least my future was no longer bleak; I had something to look forward to. What are you looking forward to?

What Pathway Are You On?

I once read that before the establishment of civilizations, there were no roads or highways. However, the animals used their survival instincts to help them find their way. They traveled several directions over and over searching for food and better living conditions. In the process, they created pathways. Over the years, people discovered those pathways and took them for the same reasons. They later became our roads and highways.

One way to make any sense out of this is to look down from an airplane's window. At ten thousand feet above ground, the highways look like a maze of tiny pathways. The pioneers of this country traveled those same pathways to settle. Later, in addition to building roads, these pioneers invented and reinvented thousands of ways to make our lives easier and better. Today, survival is no longer an issue. We are striving for what the great American psychologist Abraham Maslow calls self-actualization—the desire to become what one is capable of becoming. No matter where you may be at this point in your life, you are probably on some kind of pathway created by someone else. Which pathway is it? Where do you think this path will ultimately lead you? Are you satisfied with the direction in which you are now heading?

There are times when you must ask yourself, "Am I headed in the right direction?" Many people live life unconsciously. They have no clue where they are, or even worse, where they are going. The word future is not in their vocabulary. When I arrived in America, I expected my life to automatically become better because I realized where I was—the land of opportunity. I saw an exciting future ahead of me. I saw thousand of pathways littered with signs that said, "Opportunity." Are you familiar with those signs and pathways? It's very easy to miss them when the place becomes too familiar to you. I drove to work for seven years taking the same route every day. On that route, there were so many things I never noticed until a friend who was visiting started pointing them out to me. Has that ever happened to you? Do you remember seeing a house or building going up when all along, you never noticed there was vacant land there?

My expectations motivated me to read books, which in turn helped me to find winning pathways. What are your expectations? Answer this question with clarity, and you will find that your heart's desires will begin to draw closer to you. We all have expectations; but some of us have dismal expectations, and we often get what we expect.

My friend Jewel Daniels Radford, founder and CEO of Black Business Professionals and Entrepreneurs, is a young woman who is very clear about her expectations. She uses her high energy to work day and night putting together one of the most successful conferences for African American professionals in the world. Jewel is highly confident. She expects to win. She is a market maker. She connects the people at the bottom with those at the top so that both parties benefit. When you know for sure where you are going, maintain high expectations, and stay focused, you will connect with the right people—the Jewels of the world. You will find yourself on the right pathway every time. Your life will begin to transform.

Beyond Rice And Chicken

The first time I heard about America was when Mrs. Andre's son, Henry, returned from a visit there and told me about it. I remember sitting at his feet as he told me story after story about how good Americans had it. He talked about Disneyland, Hollywood, and Manhattan. He also said there was plenty of rice and chicken in America. I was very impressed, particularly when Henry told me about the food. At the time I was literally eating crumbs while some Haitians were basking in abundant wealth. Rice and chicken were luxury items not only for my family but also for many, many other poor Haitians as well. Maman cooked some rice on Sundays, and once a month she would cook a little chicken; but there was never enough to go around.

Between what Henry had told me about America, and the kindness and the generosity of the American tourists, a dream was born in my heart. I wanted to go to America to eat lots of rice and chicken and make something of my life. What is your dream? What people, things, or events have influenced your dreams?

Once I saw the pathways to success in America, I had bigger and better dreams. Today, my dream is crystal clear: to create such an intense emotional impact in the lives of millions of people that it will cause them to wake up! I want to be a part of something that is bigger than myself—something that will outlast my life. I want to touch future generations through my books, articles, tapes, and videos. Simply put, I want to touch the future. That is why I am so enthusiastic about my dream. What about you? Right now, what is your grandest dream?

Deep down inside of you, you know that you are worth much more than what you now have in your life. You must be able to dream beyond what your eyes can see. You have to be your own fortuneteller. What's more, you can't just think you are worth more and deserve more; you have to do something about it. Can't you tell I am excited about the direction in which I am headed? What about you?

The Pathway To America

Playing theatre in a small Catholic Church turned out to be a good thing for me. Had it not been for that, I wouldn't have met Mr. Rodriguez. It was a tiny pathway that led me to a bigger one. Mr. Rodriguez got every one of us a Canadian visa. I could hardly sleep the night before the trip. I tossed and turned thinking about the airplane and the prospects of a better and brighter life.

There is a saying in my country, "Zombie goute sel", which means zombies—people killed by having a voodoo spell put on them—don't have souls until you feed them salt. I felt the same way when I got to Montreal. I got a good taste of what living in an abundant country was like. Montreal is one of the nicest cities in the world. One can get very comfortable in such a nice city, but Canada was not going to be my last stop. I had imagined a life in America. Let me ask you a question. Are you so comfortable with where you are now that you have forgotten your original ambition or desire?

As you can tell by now, when I say pathways, I don't mean little side streets in your neighborhood; I'm talking about opportunities. Like many immigrants, I saw opportunities everywhere in America. I have asked you this question before, but I want to ask you again. What do you see and have that you are not taking advantage of? Look with fresh eyes and a sense of wonder like I did when I arrived in this country, and you will see opportunities in the least expected places. Our lives are a maze of both tiny and giant pathways. Every time you and I receive help from others, we've been shown a pathway. The books, articles, and ideas we build upon, and the people we meet are all pathways. But beware. Some pathways can lead you to a life of gratification and enjoyment; others have the potential to destroy your spirit. You must choose your pathways carefully.

Becoming A Pathmaker

I've had many people tell me that they don't have any opportunities or pathways in their life. I doubt this very strongly. When there seems to be no pathways, clear the bushes and create your own opportunity, despite the obstacles you may be facing! This is when you are called upon to be a pathmaker instead of a pathfinder. That's exactly what all the early settlers to America and other countries did—they made many of their own pathways. You can too!

I am not suggesting that creating or finding pathways to a successful life is easy. There is a tremendous price to pay. You must be willing to start from scratch and suffer disappointments, embarrassments, and setbacks. There will be some dark nights. However, when your commitment is deep enough and you are inspired enough, you will walk the narrow, dangerous pathways even when you are alone in the dark. You will stumble, but you will get up again and again. You will succeed because it's your right. You can't deny yourself that right.

Whatever It Takes

After a few performances in Canada, I ran away. I had already decided not to return to Haiti. I knew I was close to the land of my dreams and the only thing stopping me was the border! I could have stayed in Canada, but they have no tolerance for illegal immigrants. Besides, America was on my mind. I was racing ahead towards a better life. No border could stop me from reaching my dream. There was no doubt that the pathway to America was my only option. Have you ever felt that way about success? Is your dream so heavy on your mind that no border will stop you from reaching it?

However, I didn't just run immediately across the border into the United States. During the summer of 1983, while I was still in Montreal, I asked many people plenty of questions to make sure I understood how I could make my way to the United States. Someone told me of a pathway I could take. He warned me that the trip would be dangerous, but my deep desire to enter the land of my dreams was bigger than any danger. That gentleman introduced me to a Canadian lady, Mireille, who could smuggle me into America. I must admit, when I found out about the trip's details, I became very nervous! However, knowing what I knew about life in Haiti, I was ready to do whatever it took. Five days later I was on my way to America!

If I had been nervous before the trip, I was especially nervous during the trip. Prior to my departure, I had heard on the news that dead immigrants had been found in the bushes near the border. The news reporter said that truck drivers had murdered those immigrants. It dawned on me that a *truck driver was supposed to smuggle me!* I remember thinking to myself, *"What in the world was I thinking when I agreed to take that trip?"* Have you ever felt the urge to go for something, but then a little voice in your head keeps whispering, "Don't do it?" That little voice in my head was not whispering; it was screaming, "Danger!"

Back in the eighties, truck drivers traveled in pairs to avoid being caught smuggling people. The first driver would have a standard load of goods. The second driver would have goods, plus one or two people. If the Immigration and Naturalization Service officials were being particularly aggressive in inspecting the first truck's load, that driver would alert the driver behind. Some truck drivers would turn around in the dark and drop the immigrants off near the border. Others, out of fear of being caught, simply killed their illegal passengers!

As you can imagine, I had mixed emotions about entering the United States like this. On one hand, I was exhilarated because my dream was so near. On the other hand, I was extremely scared. Mireille arrived to pick me up at eleven thirty at night. As she drove, she instructed me on what I needed to do to assist the truck driver. I was allowed to bring with me only two shirts and one pair of pants in a tiny suitcase.

When we reached the pickup point, Mireille pulled into a dark corner and quietly signaled me to get out. She introduced me to the driver who was to take me. The driver walked with me to the back of the tractor-trailer and explained to me once more what Mireille had already told me. This time it was real. I saw my hiding place. The driver instructed me to start pushing myself back feet first underneath the trailer and between the rear tires until I was flat on my hands face down. Up to that point, the little voice inside my head kept telling me, "This is too dangerous! You need to back out!" Man, I was really confused, disoriented and afraid.

Before we left, Mireille told me that I would have to stay in the push-up position for about five hours before I could join the driver in the front seat. "Five hours!" I said to myself. Then she added, "The drivers have a tendency to drive fast. Make sure you hold onto the metal bar strongly." She then whispered a few words to the driver. I didn't hear what she said, but now, I was even more nervous. "Have a safe trip," Mireille told me. I said to myself, *"How could I have a safe trip when I am wedged between the rear tires of a truck?"*

Have you ever been in a position when you couldn't scratch your body? Guess what? That's exactly when every part of your body itches. That's how I felt underneath that tractor-trailer. There was no room to move; I was covered with ashes, dust and smoke; and Mireille was right—the truck driver drove fast. He didn't care that I was between the axles enduring all the shocks. I couldn't open my eyes and I had a tough time breathing because of all the smoke and dust.

All I could do was pray; and, yes, I did pray. "Dear God, please help me make it to America. I promise you I will do something meaningful with my life." The thought crossed my mind several times to simply let go and drop dead, but I had too many people in the village counting on me to help them. Plus, I had my survival instincts from poverty and diseases that urged me to hold on. I had walked dangerous pathways before, but I was not expecting such a mean pathway to America. However, that was only a fraction of the price I had to pay.

I soon discovered how much I hated being an illegal immigrant. It was embarrassing and humiliating. I spent months dodging the police or anyone in a uniform that looked like the police, including security officers. I was always watching over my back wondering if or when I'd get caught. It was maddening. I knew I couldn't continue like this forever. I came very close to going back to my country—of turning my back on my dream and on the people back home who were counting on me to make it. What could I do?

Have you ever done something wrong that you needed to make right? Are you walking around with guilt? Don't let past mistakes keep you from becoming who you were destined to be. You can make things right. Here is what you can do:

1) *Acknowledge your wrongs and forgive yourself.*

You must have the courage to admit that you did something wrong. Don't ignore the truth. Be honest with yourself and face the issue. You can never embrace your future until you rightfully settle your past. However, once you acknowledge your wrongs, you must be willing to forgive yourself. Carrying around a boatload of guilt isn't going to accomplish anything. If life were like computer software, we would all hit the undo button as many times as we are allowed. Since that isn't so, the best you can do is to forgive yourself for the wrong you've done. Then, as much as possible, you have to try and make things right.

2) *Do what you can to right the wrong.*

This is the tough part. Sometimes the past can't be fixed. But many of us simply use that line as an excuse. It's possible that your wrong may be made right if you simply offer an apology to a friend or admit that you were wrong to a co-worker; but it's often a lot more complicated than that, I know. Yes, there may be some risk involved; but a life free of guilt has to be better than the alternative. Just make sure you employ wisdom. Advice from a wise friend may help. In my case, the fix was easy. I decided to stop living in the shadows and become an American citizen. What can you do today to fix your situation?

3) Embrace Your Future And Go On To Contribute

Again, don't let past mistakes keep you from becoming who you were destined to be. Don't let them blind you to the many opportunities you have along the journey to enrich the lives of others. Every time I receive letters or emails from the people whose lives I have impacted through my writing and speaking, I know I am making things right; I know that I am making a contribution. Opportunities are everywhere. Once the guilt is gone, you will see them more clearly. Embrace the future and make a contribution.

Take Calculated Risks

To expand our lives, we often must take calculated risks. I knew I had a 98 percent chance of making it to America alive. Yet when I agreed to hang at the bottom of that truck, even though the odds were in my favor, I knew I was rolling the dice and betting everything I had on the outcome. I am not asking you to take such a drastic risk. I am simply asking you to give up something you are now enjoying in order to get what you want. Step out of your comfort zone and do something!

Exercise

- What's the biggest risk you've ever taken? How did it turn out?

- Think of a calculated risk that you've been thinking about but haven't yet attempted. What is this risk, and what can you do to overcome your hesitancy and take this risk?

It's Not About Being Smart!

Who I am today is not a measure of how much smarter I am than anybody else; it's a reflection of my drive, ambition, and insatiable appetite for knowledge. All of these give me the impetus to take risks. Everyone has the same opportunity, but there are two major diseases out there that will kill you if you're not careful. They are 1) Get rich quick and 2) Get something for nothing. Both are very contagious. It's very possible to accomplish much in this country if you are willing to pay the price, or if you are willing to walk the dangerous pathways. We can't play a game unless we are willing to risk losing. Therefore, we will have to take some risks if we are going to play the game we call life.

Exercise:

1) Think about your dream. What is it that you have no doubt in your mind you can do? I mean something that is truly who you are. Without it, your life has very little significance. It's the center of your joy. Can you think of something? Put this on paper.

2) Make a list of all your family members, friends and acquaintances—even those with whom you have not kept in touch. Place a check mark by the names of the people who you think can offer you a pathway to your dream. At first, you might feel like a you are simply using them, but remember that you are doing this because you want to make a difference in the lives of those with whom you come in contact. One day, others will call upon you for what you can do for them.

3) List other possible pathways that can help you achieve your dream. For example, does a certain city come to mind when you consider your dream? Is there a job you might take, not so much for the money as for the learning experience? Are there books, associations, etc., that might prove helpful in reaching your goal?

Once you finish with this exercise, start exploring a pathway or two. Take action now. It can be something as simple as picking up the phone to call on one of those people whose names you wrote down. I just shared my ideas with you. Perhaps they won't work for you, but you are creative enough to come up with lots of pathways that can propel you toward your heart's desire.

A Final Note

Back in the village, when the fruit was hanging on the limb of the tree, I had to risk falling in order to reach that fruit. You, too, must risk falling by reaching for the fruit. Remember: if we are not risking, we are not advancing. Whenever I feel stuck in the rut, I know I am not stretching myself. I am stagnant. The business (or person) that isn't growing is not trying new things. Like the old cliché goes: "no pain, no gain."

CHAPTER SEVEN

Be Committed, Not Just Interested!

Be Committed, Not Just Interested!

"Nothing in the world can take the place of persistence. Talent will not; nothing is more common than unsuccessful men with talent. Genius will not; unrewarded genius is almost a proverb. Education will not; the world is full of educated derelicts. Persistence and determination alone are omnipotent."
—Calvin Coolidge

Have you ever met people who are so bright, educated and talented, yet they are struggling to survive? Do you ever wonder what's wrong with these people? The answer more often than not is one simple word: Commitment. My friend, there are many people who are interested in many things, yet they are not committed to any one thing. They are always catching a new train. They never stay with anything long enough to see good results. I've heard it said that one committed person is more powerful than a hundred people who are just interested. What about you? Are you *interested*—or *committed*?

Candidly, I have failed many times throughout my life. The most powerful lesson I have learned through my failures is that nothing great happens until a person makes a total commitment to achieving a particular goal. I usually failed because I quit too early. I expected success too fast. I was simply interested. Does this sound familiar to you?

Making a commitment is the hardest thing to do. Have you ever met people who tell you that they intend to do something soon, such as start a business or go back to school? You can always tell that they are merely interested—not committed—by watching what they do. You cannot be committed to a goal when you consistently do things that have nothing to do with that goal. Am I right?

When I made up my mind to become a professional speaker, I had already learned about the power of commitment. I made a vow to stick to my plan until I succeeded. Since day one, the business was very challenging for me. There were times when I thought about quitting. Money was very scarce, and I faced language and other barriers that could have prevented me from pursuing my dream. I refused to quit. It is hard to stay in a business that is not bringing income when you can't afford to put food on your table. Well, that is precisely what commitment is all about.

If you are thinking about quitting because things are too slow or challenges beyond your control keep showing up, you need to think about it again. Life tends to reward those who stay in the ring long enough to endure the blows. I've said this before, but I think it bears repeating again here: the people at the top of any field are not necessarily those who are the smartest; they are those who are committed. Think back to a time when you were moving toward a particular goal, and you quit before you succeeded. Do you now believe that you would have achieved that goal had you persisted? I bet you would have.

I've heard some people say things like, "I'm not smart enough," or "I don't think I can do this because I don't have the right education." What do people mean anyway when they say, "being smart?" There are many requirements to success, but education is definitely not one of them—although it can surely speed up the process. It's nice to be educated, but it's even nicer to have a good dose of common sense and a little creativity. The people who are very successful in this world are not those with advanced degrees. If you don't believe me, go to your local bookstore or library and read some biographies. I guarantee you, for every person with multiple degrees and advanced schooling, there are 19 others who don't have those things.

Personally, I don't even believe in being smart. "Smart" is a relative term. Instead, I believe in common sense, ambition, and, of course, unswerving commitment. To me, the greatest sin in the world is to deny others the opportunity to prove themselves because of their lack of education. A person who is ambitious, committed, and creative, and a person who wants to try something new in spite of his or her fears will always get my vote. I only pity those who are not willing to take risks and learn. For the record, I do believe in learning. I strongly advocate getting a formal education, but lack of education alone isn't a sufficient barrier to success. Don't let the absence of a formal degree handicap you. Besides, if you can read, you can educate yourself.

You Gotta Give It All You've Got: Making The Investment

A few years after I arrived in America, I read the book See You At The Top, by Zig Ziglar. At the end of the book Zig wrote, "See you at the top!" At the time, I had no idea where I would be when I finally met Zig at the top, yet I also knew that in America anything was possible. Several years went by and I forgot about his words. In the meantime, I tried my hands at many things in my pursuit of the American Dream. Finally, I discovered that my calling in life is to provide strategies for those who are stuck at the bottom so that they can move to the top. With a burning desire and the willingness to give it my all, I set out to become a motivational speaker. I decided to follow the pathways of the highly successful master motivators.

"Hi, Sir. My name is Rene Godefroy. I am a doorman now and I am from a small village in Haiti. My dream is to become a motivational speaker like you, Sir. Who knows, one day we will share a platform." Those were my words to many of the motivational speakers who came through the doors of the Renaissance Waverly

No Condition Is Permanent! *by Rene Godefroy*

Hotel in Atlanta, Georgia, as they checked into the hotel. On many occasions, at 11:00 p.m., when my co-workers were heading home, I headed straight to the ballroom where they had set up for the next morning's keynote speaker. I would stand on the platform and claim the "audience" as mine and give my speech to an empty room. The chairs weren't very responsive, of course, but I was programming my subconscious for the realization of my dream. Occasionally, others saw me and thought I was going crazy. One guy asked me, "Man, are you losing it? You are talking to yourself!" I said, "I'm not losing it; I'm building it!"

Some of the speakers I met took me very seriously when I introduced myself to them as the doorman who would become a motivational speaker. Others weren't very responsive. One of my goals was to attend a National Speakers Association conference. Since I was not a member, I would have to pay the full fee to attend. I didn't have the cash, so I began saving all of my tip money until I had enough to attend my first conference. I gave up a lot in order to get what I wanted. All of my money went into learning what I needed to know to make my dream come true. Now, let me ask you this: what investments or sacrifices are you willing to make in the next six months to achieve your dream?

I had been told that if one wanted to significantly reduce the learning curve required to break into the speaking arena, one only had to join the National Speakers Association. The first NSA conference I attended was in Anaheim, California. I couldn't afford a room at the hotel where the conference was being held, but that didn't matter as long as I was there. I would have loved to rub shoulders with the "pros" in the evening, but I had to rush back to my hotel to review my notes and get some sleep. There was a lot to learn. I was overwhelmed!

"Hi, Sir, my name is Rene—your doorman from Atlanta, Georgia. Do you remember me, Sir? I told you I was going to be a speaker. Here I am!" That's how I went around introducing myself to the speakers for whom I had served as a doorman during their visits to the Atlanta hotel. I could see the "*Wow!*" look on their faces. They were so proud of me because I had demonstrated that I wasn't merely *interested* in speaking; I was *committed*.

Keep Coming Back Again And Again

Dan Burrus, who is such an incredible human being, was so impressed to see me. He pulled me into a corner and said, "Son, there is no doubt in my mind you are definitely serious. I encourage you to keep coming back again and again." I can still hear Dan's voice talking to me. He was very sincere. He went on to tell me that when Les Brown (now one of America's most renowned motivational speakers) came to his first NSA convention, he was so broke that he had to borrow money for the bus trip home! Not long after that, Les arrived in a Leer Jet as one of the keynote speakers for the National Speakers Association.

During my first NSA conference, Dan was the only big time speaker who gave me a lot of his time. I once heard a saying that you can always tell a big person by the way he or she treats little people. To me, Dan is a giant! What's more, I followed his advice. I devoted all my time and resources to mastering my craft. I learned everything that I could about speaking about the business aspects of the profession, and about the audiences' needs and wants. I attended every convention I could, even when money was scarce.

After my third convention, something magical happened to me: Thanks to Mark Mayberry, I was invited to be the keynote speaker at the National Speakers Association conference in Washington, DC. I couldn't believe it! I entitled my keynote, "Beyond My Wildest Dreams!" Can you guess who was going to share the platform with me? Zig Ziglar, the man who told me at the end of his book that he'd see me at the top. I also remembered Dan telling me how Les Brown had showed up in a Leer Jet for his keynote presentation. Well, I didn't have a Leer Jet, so I did one better than that. I showed up in a Delta 747.

Build On Your Successes

After I keynoted the conference, many of the new speakers in attendance instantly saw me as an "expert". However, that was their perception of me. I have never considered myself to be an expert in the field. I am a student. The newcomers asked me lots of questions. Many were surprised that I was invited to speak at such an early stage in my career. They all wanted to know my secret for being so effective on the platform, especially given that I was a relatively "new kid" on the block. I must give credit to many people for my big break, especially to Mark for taking my demo video to the board of the NSA. Yet, in the end, I told the new speakers that I had succeeded because I had given it all that I could. Somehow others sensed and felt my commitment. I was dead serious about making it to the top along with the seasoned speakers.

Obtaining meaningful and significant success is serious business. It is nothing to play with. Yes, you can have fun along the way, but it isn't something to joke about. Success is always looking for people who are serious about becoming successful; being half-hearted is not the way to go. Only commitment will do. When I discovered that speaking was my calling, I wrote down my plan and resolved to commit to it, no matter what. Do you have a solid plan, one that's written down? What will you do in the next few days, weeks, and months that will put you a few steps closer to your dream?

Many people say to me, "I can't succeed alone—I need some help." Unfortunately, you won't get much help from others when you begin. You must have the mentality that you are going to do it all by yourself. Then help will show up when you least expect it. Why? It is because help is only available to those who have a solid plan backed by solid commitment. Others are not going to waste time with you if they think you are only interested. Just as investors don't invest money in a company that is unstable, people don't invest time in an idea that's not backed by passion, a strong commitment, and a solid plan.

Over time, as your commitment continues, help will come. Today, for example, I am very lucky to have access to movers and shakers with whom I can consult at no charge. The key, of course, is for you to continue no matter what. Make your investment of time up front, and soon others will match it. Commitment and preparation are the hinges upon which success swings. What's more, you can control both of these attributes.

Preparing Versus Hoping And Wishing

If opportunity stops by your door and knocks, can you get up and go, or will you need time to prepare yourself? What a daring question! When I received the call to keynote the NSA conference, I had been preparing myself for four years. Until then, I didn't know the first thing about the magnitude of what would come my way. Had I not been prepared, I would have bombed big time, and that first impression in front of my peers would have lasted forever.

I can't state enough how critical preparation is to your success. I have already mentioned that I discovered many pathways to success in America. However, I also realized that I needed a great deal of preparation to best take advantage of those various opportunities. I wasted no time and got busy doing what I believed I needed to do to succeed. There are those who desire to get to the next level, yet they are doing nothing to prepare for the next opportunity. They hope and wish that somehow things will fall into place. Wrong!

I once saw a bumper sticker that said, "The Best Never Rest." You and I know that if we are going to strive to be the very best in our field, we can't rest. Life is a race. The moment you blink, millions pass you by. The main goal is to continually acquire news strategies to help you run the race a little faster. Whether the desire is for a promotion or for improving the bottom line of your department or business, you have to continually prepare your mind to face the challenges ahead. Preparation is the only way you can face your tomorrows. Are you ready for your big break, or will you need more time to prepare when it comes?

Commitment and preparation go hand in hand. In fact, we must make a commitment to commitment itself. Then commitment will force us to discipline ourselves to learn and prepare. When I keynoted at the National Speakers Association, some people marveled at my "sheer talent" for speaking. I am really not too big on talent. The bottom line is that when I want to achieve phenomenal results, I commit and prepare. I know some people just show up and try to wing it, but I am not one of those people.

Watch Out For Distractions

The moment you commit to a goal or dream, you will find all kinds of distractions along the way. One of the things I always advise young people to do is to learn to identify and isolate possible distractions. So many things are competing for your attention that it can literally be impossible to focus on a task unless you consciously filter out the fluff. There are many around us who could be playing professional sports, acting on the big screen or singing on stage. Instead, they are walking around emotionally wounded because they know they had enough talent to make it big, but didn't. Why? They got distracted.

Early in my speaking career, I had friends who tried their best to distract me, though they didn't know that's what they were doing. They only knew that if I wasn't going out to party and chase women, something must have been wrong with me. Little did they know I was shaping and creating my future. What are your distractions? Are they your friends, family members, or a romantic interest? One young lady once told me that she is so in love, she can't even focus on her goals. I suppose she is using her heart instead of her head. Let me share with you some strategies to help you stay committed and prepare yourself for success.

Four Steps To Prepare Yourself

"A mind once stretched by a new idea never regains its original dimension."—Oliver Wendell Holmes

Step One: Become An Expert In Your Field
Would you like to have an edge over the people in your field? When was the last time you read either a book or a magazine (pertaining to your field) cover to cover? How much more do you know now than you knew five years ago? What does your personal inventory of skills and talents look like? Can you convince your boss to give you a raise based on your accumulated knowledge of your field? Are you an expert? If you own a business, are you advancing confidently because you've learned so much about ways to positively impact your bottom line?

If you answered 'yes' to all these questions, congratulations—your future is unlimited! If you answered 'no' to two or more of these questions, chances are that your car is in neutral. Don't feel bad. All of us slip every now and then. That is precisely why we are engaging in this conversation. My goal is to help you get back on track.

The mind is like a leaky bucket: it is constantly dripping information. Unless we are constantly adding more, we will soon wake up and find ourselves empty and useless. Consider this: How much of what you learned in high school can you still remember today? Better yet, how much of this conversation will you remember later? Not much. What that means is that you have to learn a lot in order to fill your mind with usable skills. Does that make sense to you? From this moment on, make a commitment to be the very best in your field by learning all there is to learn about it. If you want your salary to increase, you had first better learn more. Like I always say, "The level of your purse will always rise to meet the level of your mind. If you want to flood your purse, you have to first flood your mind!"

Read Books
How often do you read? The late Earl Nightingale, a pioneer in the area of self-help, said that if we read one hour a day on any specific subject, in five years we would become a national expert; in ten years we would have the equivalent of a Ph.D. Anyone can fol-

low Mr. Nightingale's advice, but it would require tremendous self-discipline. You might not be able to study one subject every day for one hour for five or ten years, but you can certainly try. Many people graduate from high school or college and say to themselves, "Thank God I am through with school. I will never open another book!" Wrong! School never ends. A graduation is merely the beginning of our learning journey. That is why they call the graduation ceremony the commencement ceremony. It is the beginning of learning.

You might say, "I don't have time to read. By the time I get out of work, I have to take care of a thousand things." All you are telling me is that you are not serious about reaching the top of your field. Time is completely relative. We never have the time to do anything. We must make the time! We must sacrifice a little to get a lot. Have you ever heard of books on tape? Have you ever considered banning television from your home? That may be the choice you will have to make to be able to nurture your future.

Get a Thirty-Year Education In One Month
I can hear someone saying, "How can that be possible?" It's very easy, and I'm not talking about peripheral knowledge; I'm talking about specific and useable ideas that can make a significant difference in your life. Let's say you bought a book by business and management expert, Tom Peters, or one by an expert in your field. Do you realize that the author has condensed thirty or more years of his best knowledge into only two to three hundred pages? What if you could digest every one of his ideas and use them? It would cost you approximately $25. Is it possible to get thirty years of education anywhere for $25? I don't think so! Do you? This is what is called OPE = Other People's Experience. It sounds like an easy concept, doesn't it? Why, then, do so few people read books? Did you know that ninety percent of all the books are read by only ten percent of the population?

Read Magazines And Newsletters
Another idea is to subscribe to every magazine in your field and

read them. What if you don't have time? No problem. Buy sub-scriptions for your friends with the understanding they will share with you the ideas and stories they learn. It's not a bad deal. Your friends get a free subscription to a magazine in their field to feed their minds, and all they have to do in return is share what they learn with you. I know people who pay others to read books and magazines for them. They receive a written report in return. Depending on how much your time is worth, you might even pay a retired schoolteacher to read for you. Call the high schools in your area and ask them to put you in touch with some retirees. There is always a way!

Step Two: Join An Association

My strongest piece of advice for you would be to join the main association in your field. I owe both the National Speakers Association and its local chapter in Georgia a big debt for my suc-cess. Yes, I could have learned everything I now know without these organizations, but it would have taken me years of fumbling around in the dark. Call your association and join today. You will reduce your learning curve tremendously. If you're currently employed, your company will almost certainly foot the bill for you. Don't think that there is no association that is in some way related to your field. In America, regardless of what you do, there is an association dedicated to sharing and empowering its mem-bers with cutting-edge knowledge. It cost me a great deal of money to keep my membership in different associations, but I believe it would have been much more expensive not to have become a member.

How To Benefit From Your Association

Of course, joining an association means nothing unless you are willing to become an active member. You will know the size of your commitment to a thing by observing the quantity and quality of time you spend on that thing. Having joined my association, I attended its meetings religiously. There were times when I could have been somewhere else, but I chose to attend the meetings. You can tell I was committed. Ask yourself this question: "By spending my time doing this, am I investing my time or am I spending it?" You and I both know that there is a big difference between an expense and an investment. We also both know that the choices you make today about where you spend your time will directly affect your future.

Your involvement in the association should also give you opportunities to practice meeting other people in your field. The first few meetings I attended, no one knew me; and although many members went out of their way to acknowledge me, I still felt somewhat like a stranger. Thankfully, I understood that every pathway has its bumps. I took the initiative and began introducing myself to as many people as I could. I also volunteered to assist others. Over the course of several months, I volunteered as co-director of logistics, and then as co-director of the speakers' showcase. I helped with organizing our annual speakers' school, and I also volunteered for the meet and greet committee. Finally, I sat on the nominating committee. Pretty soon a funny thing happened. Everyone knew me by first name. In less than two years I had gone from being a newcomer to being a veteran! What about you? Have you volunteered for your organization lately? You can become a household name in your association in no time by volunteering on different committees.

Step Three: Become A Small Fish In A Big Pond

Would you like to hang with the big boys? Have you ever wondered how you can become a small fish in a big pond? Would you like to meet your potential employers, clients, or customers? By now you should know the answer: join an association! I have always wanted to meet the movers and shakers in my industry—people who could open some doors for me.

You might ask, "I already have a job in my area of interest. Do I really need to go through so much trouble?" I've got news for you, my friend; there's no guarantee that your job will be there tomorrow. We are living in a time when things are changing at breakneck speed. Your company can let you go in a moment's notice. The remarkable thing is even the company president or CEO may not know what's going to happen. Like the saying goes in my country, "Don't wait until you are sleepy to make your bed up—it will be too late." Network with your peers now. You never know; your next job might come from one of them.

If you are in sales, you already know that it's difficult to talk to the actual buyer. You can only get as far as the company's gate-keepers. If you want to get beyond the front doors, you must attend networking events. There are many highly respected authors and speakers to whom I would never have had access had I not become an NSA member.

Let me give you an example. Jeffrey Gitomer is one of the most respected sales gurus in the world. His column appears daily in business journals across the country and in some columns across the world. I was very familiar with Jeffrey's work, and I had always wanted to meet him.

As a doorman, I always wanted to know what the people at the top were reading. The moment I noticed a book on the back seat of the car I was parking, I would run to Barnes and Nobles across the street and buy that book. How is that for commitment? One day, Jeffrey pulled up at the hotel. I noticed that he had a stack of his book, The Sales Bible. He shook my hand and said, "My name is Jeffrey Gitomer, and I have a tip for you. The choice is yours. Will it be a book or five dollars?" I answered, "The book!" After that meeting with Jeffrey, I wanted to stay in touch.

Jeffrey was a big fish in a big pond, and I was a small fish. Later, I joined the National Speakers Association, and, lo and behold, Jeffrey was a member! Hello! He and I became friends. Did you read the foreword to this book? Jeffrey wrote it, of course. Do you get my point? Of course you do. You can get to know the people at the top by simply becoming a member of your industry's association.

Step Four: Become Computer Proficient

You may be surprised to find out that many people are clueless when it comes to computers. It's been said that there are three groups of people: The first group makes things happen, the second stands by and watches things happen, and the third group keeps asking, "What happened?" Unfortunately, many belong to the third group. They are the ones who look at you with a blank look on their faces when you mention a computer term. They don't even know the basics. Most resist computers with all their might. The reality is that we can no longer get ahead without using some kind of computer. I hope you are one who embraces them.

In 1983 when I arrived in this country, personal computers hadn't yet been introduced. A few short years later, the first real wave of technology began to carry us to a new, high-tech world. Suddenly computers were becoming a necessity. Although I was in the process of learning English, I made a decision to surf with the wave. Some people thought computers were a fad. Others categorically refused to have anything to do with them, but my curiosity caused me to join the high-tech revolution rather than avoid it. Are you computer literate, or are you still resisting?

My very first computer was an AT model. Later, when the 286 machines came on the market, I bought one. Yes, I was afraid, just like many people. In those days, you had to memorize lots of commands in order to use a computer. It wasn't easy, especially for me; but as I have already mentioned, the future does not belong to the smartest and most talented; it belongs to those who commit and take risks in spite of their fears.

Today, I am not only computer literate, but I am also computer proficient. I discovered that my computer skills came in very handy when I started in the speaking arena. Of course, I can now afford to pay somebody to do the work for me; but early on my computer knowledge saved me a lot of money. I built my first web site when many veteran speakers did not even have a website up. I have also received lots of compliments about the marketing materials I created. In fact, to this day, before I turn over any graphic work to a graphic artist, I choose to do the first design layout. I am able to do so because of my basic computer skills. If you are not very good with computers, you should seriously consider taking some courses to bring you up to speed. You will be astounded at how much you can accomplish with a PC or laptop. It doesn't matter how long you resist, you will one day be required to go high-tech—and soon. In the new digital frontier, you will need to have some type of computer skills just to use the household appliances. Why not choose to be proactive? You have everything to gain and nothing to lose. How's that for a risk-free investment?

Step Five: Turn Your Car Into A University On Wheels

What do you listen to in your car on a regular basis? I don't know about your city, but traffic in Atlanta, Georgia, is tough. It seems like the more lanes they add to the highway, the more congested traffic becomes. You and I will spend an enormous amount of time on the road during our lifetime. That's OK. We can leverage our time by educating ourselves. It's incredible how much educational material there is available on audiocassettes and CDs. We can turn our automobile into a university on wheels.

There are more radio stations today than ever. That translates into more music and more advertising. It's easy to get distracted. I encourage you to invest the time you'd normally spend listening to the radio by instead listening to educational and motivational audio products. For many years, I have ordered products from Nightingale-Conant. I have listened to some of the best advice, strategies, and biographies while in my car. Today, the return on my investment has grown a thousand fold. What about you? If I were to look around your car, would I notice some educational tapes? How committed are you?

One Last Thing

I am glad you spent the time to engage in this discussion with me about commitment— about feeding your mind. I hope you don't just stop there. Now I want to hear from you. I want to know what strategies you will use to commit and stay focused. I urge you not to join the ranks of those who dibble and dabble with things. Get serious! Commit to sacrificing time, energy and money to get ahead. Avoid distractions. So far, I have shared enough about myself with you to convince you of the power of commitment. The rest is up to you.

CHAPTER EIGHT

Keep Your Attitude Positively Charged

Keep Your Attitude Positively Charged

—⚮—

"Man is made or unmade by himself; in the armory of thought
he forges the weapons by which he destroys himself.
He also fashions the tools with which he builds for himself
heavenly mansions of joy and strength and peace. By the right
choice and true application of thought, man ascends to the
Divine Perfection; by the abuse and wrong application of
thought, he descends below the level of the beast. Between these
two extremes are all the grades of character, and man is
their maker and master."—James Allen

D o people get under your skin sometimes? Have you ever felt so mad that you wanted to slap somebody? If you're like the vast majority of people in the world today, the answer to both of these questions is "yes!" When you feel upset and irritated because of what someone has said or done, you are automatically giving up your power to that person. You are wasting your time and energy. Do you agree with me? You and I know full well that it is extremely difficult to ignore some people. However, you have to do just that because it is the hallmark of high achievers. You have to do that because you have class.

I believe you and I possess an incredible fortune that, if used properly, can make us happy. That fortune can also be the source of our misery. What is it? It's our attitude. You can create heaven or hell in your life depending on how you mold and shape your attitude. What is attitude anyway? It's the way we react to circumstances. You and I can make a choice right now to be happy regardless of what's going on in our lives. All we have to do is to change our attitude—the way we react to external events. To sum it up, we have to change our inner conversations, and stop relinquishing control over the way we feel based on the comments and actions of others.

On The Turn Of A Hundred Dime

When I first began working at the Waverly Hotel, I thought I was in heaven. I started as a limousine driver. I was so excited! It was my first job working for a hotel. I mean, I was on top of the world! I had free uniforms, and the hours were great. The food was FREE, and they served rice and chicken on a regular basis! Remember, rice and chicken were luxury items for me in Haiti. I said to myself, "I am going to keep this job forever. Driving a limousine, tips, a paycheck, and free food. What a country!"

After one month on the job, I was standing outside when a slender, tall, older gentleman with blond hair approached me. His face was red, and he had a hard time walking straight. I immediately noticed that he was drunk. He said to me, "I am looking for a place I can get some spirits." The term 'spirits' was a new one to me because I hadn't been in the U.S. all that long at the time. Naturally, because he was so drunk and because I didn't understand the term, I thought he was looking for repentance. I said to him, "Sir, there is a Holy Spirit church right around the corner." He snapped, "I am looking for some liquor, man!"

So I took the gentleman to the liquor store in the hotel's limousine. We arrived, and I opened the door for him and showed him where to go. He crawled out of the back seat and stumbled his way to the liquor store. I thought he was going to fall down. Today, I often wonder what would possess anyone to drink himself silly. I suppose I took him to buy the liquor because he was a guest of the hotel. Otherwise, I would have turned down his request.

Five minutes later he returned carrying a bag filled with liquor.

He shoved himself into the back of the limo. I put on my seatbelt and said, "Okay, back to the hotel." The man began screaming at me, "No, I don't want to go back to the hotel. I want to go downtown!" I said, "Sir, I am sorry. According to the hotel's policy, I can only travel within a one mile radius of the hotel." He got angry, "I don't care about the policy. I just want to go downtown." I looked at him calmly and said, "Sir, please understand; I don't want to lose my job." And I was serious. There was nothing in the world that was going to make me take this man downtown. He kept shouting and I kept reacting. The more he shouted, the more my attitude changed.

After a few exchanges with the man, he got the message that I had made up my mind not to take him downtown. He was livid. He turned all red. As soon as I buckled my seat belt and put the car in drive, I heard a whoosh sound over my shoulder. "Oh my god!" I said to myself. I looked up in my rearview mirror and saw a brand new hundred-dollar bill flying across the dashboard. I pushed the brakes and said to the gentleman, "Sir, do you want me to take 75 South or 20 West to downtown?" He said, "I don't care what you do, as long I get there!"

You bet I took him. Seeing the hundred-dollar bill flying across the dashboard took my attitude from being irritated to being extremely calm and polite. That gentleman succeeded in changing my attitude on the turn of a dime (or, in this case, on the turn of a hundred). The reality was that I gave up my power to dictate the way I feel at any given moment to a total stranger. Has that ever happened to you?

Events Are Neutral

That incident happened almost 14 years ago. Today, I am a totally changed man. Money does not motivate me as much as it did then. I have more substance and meaning in my life. I told you that story to illustrate how I gave my power of choice to a stranger I had never met before. What's even more unsettling, he was drunk, which means he didn't even have control over himself. Do you realize how that man pushed every one of my buttons? First, he got me mad; then he changed my attitude almost on cue. I had a choice. I didn't even have to exchange words with the gentleman. I could have driven him quietly back to the hotel; but, instead, I continued to exchange words with him back and forth. When was the last time you quietly walked away from an argument? It takes a powerful person to be able to do so.

You might say, "Come on Rene, if you knew who I have to deal with every day, you would understand why I get so upset some-times." I am not disputing the fact that some people can really tick you off. I am saying, though, that you can make a conscious deci-sion to process what happens to you differently. It's not what hap-pens to us (events) that matter most; it's what we say to ourselves that either makes us mad or happy. The man at the hotel was very drunk. I am sure if I met him today, he would not even remember what he said. I could easily have said, "He is drunk. I will pay no mind to him." The reality is that we always have choices regarding how we will think, what we will feel or what we will do about a sit-uation. We just need to learn to keep those choices in perspective.

Think about it. Most of your frustrations are really simply a matter of attitude—the things you are saying to yourself on a con-sistent basis. Many of us are so frustrated with our current posi-tion, yet we continue to make the same choices again and again. We get into relationships that cause us to shrink instead of grow, yet we continue to stay. Our inner conversations keep causing us to build up anger until we finally explode. Does this sound famil-iar to you? The best way to deal with such situations is to shift your focus—your attitude—from 'I am stuck' to 'I am capable of handling this situation with elegance'. It's incredible how we can use the awesome power of words to adjust our attitude. We are only stuck when we believe we are. Consciously change your inner conversations and you will change your world.

When Your Shell Is Too Tight, Get Out!

Do you sometimes feel your life is like a treadmill? It seems like you are moving very fast, yet you are still in the same place. Are you in a relationship that you wish you had never gotten into? Do you feel underpaid and overworked? If you answer 'yes' to any of these questions, you have outgrown your shell. It's time to make a move, and all it takes is to simply change your attitude. As long you spend all of your energy cursing your current life, you will always find yourself in the same situation.

I want to share with you a pearl of wisdom I learned while living in my village. Have you ever heard of hermit crabs? They are like any other crab. They have large and small teeth. They live in shells. The bottom part of their body is soft and coiled inside the shell, and the front part—the teeth—hangs outside the shell. To move about, the hermit crab drags its shell slowly while holding on to it with its teeth. As a kid, I was often fascinated watching the hermit crabs. I remember the day I stumbled upon a bunch of them. I squatted down and picked one up to take a good look at it. I had some questions. I wondered what happens to it once it outgrows its shell. That's a fair question for a kid to ask, don't you think? Kids are full of why's. Even as adults we still ask why except that we don't vocalize it as much.

Deeply immersed in my fascination, the hermit crab and I became one. Then a man by the name of Rafael Paul came by and asked, "What are you doing here, Son?" Startled, I quickly replied, "Nothing, Sir. I am just admiring this hermit crab and wondering what's going on in its world." I told Raphael my questions and he told me the answers. He said that the hermit crabs are very intelligent creatures. When they get too big for their shell, they look for bigger ones.

"What happens if they can't find a bigger shell?", I asked. "Well, they will continue to look until they die in frustration.", Raphael replied. He went on to say that nature always provides a shell. "Son, the most fascinating thing about the hermit crab is that it will not break or mistreat the old shell. It slowly crawls out of it." "Do you know why?", Raphael continued. "I guess its mind is too fixed on the new shell," I said. "Good answer, but it is far from the truth," Raphael replied. "The real answer is that it knows another hermit crab will find that old shell to be the perfect home."

So my friend, here is a timeless lesson from Petite-Riviere— my village. Now, I want to ask you this. How tight is your shell? Are you in a tight shell that causes you to have a negatively charged attitude? What shell am I talking about? Well, it could be a physical shell such as a relationship; but I am also talking about a mental shell—an attitude.

There Is a Bigger Shell Somewhere

Are you in a frustrating relationship? How satisfied are you with your current position in life? Think about it. Perhaps you entered into a friendship or into a dating relationship when you were immature. You then began to grow and expand your horizons by learning more and capitalizing on your past experiences. Your partner, however, may not be growing; instead, he or she is shrinking. You try very hard to see how you can help, but nothing works. What do you do? You find a bigger shell. When you entered into the relationship, you entered into a shell. If you are expanding and the other person is contracting, that's a big problem. You will find yourself stressed and frustrated until, just like the hermit crab, you begin to die on the inside. It doesn't have to be this way. Life is too darn short!

The same is true for your work environment. Maybe you feel you aren't getting anywhere—your shell has become too small. Perhaps the first month or year on the job was very exhilarating. You were learning! Now the job is no longer challenging. There is not much to learn. You lose interest. Your attitude changes from excitement to boredom—from positive to negative. When that happens, it's time to seek a promotion within the company or look for a new job. A person with a negatively charged attitude can ruin any team, and you don't want to be that person. Be as wise as the hermit crab. Make a move!

I can hear someone saying, "I sent my résumé out five times, and I can't get a new job." Have you ever heard the old saying that life is a numbers game? That means that if you want to increase your chance of winning, you have to multiply your efforts. A typical response ratio in advertising is two percent—for every 100 people who see the ad, two might respond. It's the same with sending out your résumé. You might get two job offers if you choose to make one hundred attempts. You've got to go through the numbers. Does that make sense to you? By the way, this is positive thinking. Okay, enough about jobs. Let's get a little bit more wisdom from the hermit crab.

Don't you sometimes think that you deserve better? Here is something you might want to hear: you absolutely deserve better! The hermit crab's wisdom says, "I deserve better, and I will not settle for less. If this shell is stressing me to death, I've got to move on." However, there is one characteristic about the hermit crab that you and I should take into careful consideration. It never breaks or mistreats the old shell. The hermit crab knows the shell it leaves behind will be the perfect fit for a smaller crab. We don't have to break or mistreat our old shell, either. In other words, don't get ugly, and don't get even. There are enough people walking around with a wounded and broken heart. Those people are miserable and cause everyone with whom they come in contact to be miserable, too. You and I don't want to be a part of that. Right?

Sometimes your shell might be a mental shell. This is the time when you feel you are waiting forever for a red light to turn green. You are stuck at a dead-end. What that really means is your mental shell is too tight. Albert Einstein said, "The significant problems we are facing cannot be solved at the same level of thinking we were at when we created them." When I first arrived in America, I found myself in a brand new country and culture. I didn't speak the language, but I quickly discovered that this is the land of opportunities. I realized that I needed to change my mental shell in order to take advantage of the opportunities I saw. Simply put, I needed a new attitude. What did I do? I set out to reinvent myself—to change my old thinking so that I could solve the problems I was facing. When was the last time you reinvented or reengineered your life? Do you want a better position? How about starting your own business? Maybe it's time to reinvent yourself.

How To Be A Powerful Positive Person

In Petite Riviere—my village, I formed the essence of what has carried me this far in life. Almost everything I experienced as a child in the village gave me distinct learning opportunities for my adulthood. Well, in my village, I also learned about the bee and the rattlesnake. This story also illustrates a critical piece of wisdom to make people powerful and positive...and a leader. I'm not sharing this nugget with you for you to say, "That's nice." No, I encourage you to think of how you can apply this information, and apply it on a consistent basis until it forms the essence of who you are. It's a struggle, but every day I try to adopt the attitude I'm about to share with you. I have received countless emails and letters from my fans telling me how this concept has literally transformed their attitude overnight. Use it and you will become a powerful, positive person. Ignore it and your life will be a fog of cynical doubt and confusion. Can you feel my passion for this one? Buckle up and let's get to it!

Adopt The BEE Attitude!

A man in the village whose name I don't remember shared the Bee attitude with me. He wasn't from my village. He was merely a passerby, but he gave me a powerful gift—a metaphor for life, if you will. On the one hand, you have the bee. When a bee is out buzzing about, what is it looking for? Come on! This isn't a trick question. The answer is straightforward. The bee is looking for something sweet—the nectar. It spends an enormous amount of time sucking flowers to find sweetness. The bee needs this sweetness to make honey. You and I know the awesome nutritional value of honey. In its pure form, honey is loaded with incredible vitamins. Every waking minute and hour of the day, the bee, whether it's building the hive or working in the field, is busy preparing to create honey. What a powerful way to stay busy!

On the other hand, you have the rattlesnake. The man in the village told me that the rattlesnake is always busy doing the opposite of what the bee does. It is constantly looking for things that are bitter. The rattlesnake sucks the bitterness and uses it to create its deadly poison. He also told me that the rattlesnake survives by striking and killing living creatures. What a horrible way to stay busy!

Isn't this the same way it is with people? Some are bees, while others behave like rattlesnakes. People with a rattlesnake attitude go through life searching for bitterness. Haven't you met a rattlesnake before? Of course you have. Maybe you didn't recognize it. Don't you have people around you who are always quick to point out your shortcomings? They meet you for ten minutes, and they already pick apart all your weaknesses. They are often the town gossipers. Well, those people are rattlesnakes. They have the power to strike and destroy communities, churches, families, etc. Once you share your dream or goal with a rattlesnake, he or she injects poison into it until your dream is dead. I am telling you, it's easy to become a rattlesnake.

If you and I are going to be positive, powerful people, we need to strive for the bee attitude. Every one of us experiences moments when we suffer from lack of self-confidence, especially when there are lots of rattlesnakes around. The last thing we need is for a person to bruise our ego. If confidence creates more confidence, then you have the power to pump more self-confidence into those with whom you come in contact. Just praise the best in them. People with a bee attitude have a special way of magnifying your strengths and making you feel good. They can bring the best out of you.

You can become highly noticed when you exude the bee attitude. It sounds simple, yet it's very profound. Act like the bee and people will seek you out. The goal is to reach deep inside of others and magnify their strengths in front of them and to look for the best in every situation. Yes, it's hard to focus on the positive when so many rattlesnakes are charming you, but remember this: being a rattlesnake can be automatic; being a bee is something you have to consciously choose to do.

5 Ways To Handle Rattlesnakes Around You

Here are five ways to overcome the rattlesnakes in your life. Use these often—every day if you have to!

1) Zap them out of your life. Make a list of all the people you know, and then go down the list and ask yourself, "Do I feel better and more inspired whenever I talk to this person? Does my self-confidence go up or down?" In other words, is this person a bee or a rattlesnake? If the answer is the latter, zap him or her out of your life. Don't be harsh, however. Always think of the hermit crab. You don't have to hate or create hard feelings. Do it with grace and elegance. Be utterly diplomatic.

2) Disarm them. Marie Joe Maurice, has a wonderful way to deal with negative people. When anyone tries to tell her that someone said something negative about her, she answers, "Oh, I don't think that person would ever say that kind of mean thing about me." However, Marie Joe is fully aware that the person may have indeed said such a thing. Marie Joe told me there is a method to her madness, however. She is attempting to discourage the gossiper (rattlesnake) from striking and destroying.

3) Refuse to give them your time. Avoid spending time or having meaningful conversations with rattlesnakes. It's a total waste of your time. If you absolutely have to converse with such people, be a bee throughout the conversation. Pump up their ego and self-confidence, because whether you know it or not, these people suffer from low self-esteem.

4) Keep it positive. Never say anything negative about the people you have zapped out of your life. If they have told you a secret, it should remain a secret; don't share this information with others. Be above petty gossip. When others try to talk negatively about others, remember Marie Joe's strategy. A guy I once worked with was a very intelligent and out going person. He could connect with anyone in a heartbeat. There was one problem. He had the rattlesnake attitude. I decided to avoid him at all costs. He kept spreading rumors about me. Others warned me about him. However, I always found something good to say about him. If there wasn't anything good to say, I kept silent.

5) Advertise your BEE Attitude. Warn your friends and family members about your new BEE ATTITUDE. You might even want to explain the concept to them. Go to the extent of holding your friends and family members accountable and vice versa. Together we can rid people of the stuff that forms their poison. They will no longer be able to strike.

Don't Try To Change Them—Change Yourself

When I arrived in America, I was twenty-one years young. I had heard that there were plenty of women in this country. I met a guy in Miami by the name of Philip who knew where the action was happening. I befriended him and we started hanging out. Philip took me to a club on Biscayne Boulevard. The club's name was Big Daddy's. I know, it sounded funny to me, too. I stood there and read the sign a couple of times to confirm that I was reading it right. I was nervous and intimidated; but hey, Philip said it was the place to be.

I didn't know what to expect as we entered. It was my first time inside a disco. The music was very loud. I saw people screaming in each other's ears trying to carry on a conversation; the lights flashed at a dizzying speed. The place was packed. People stood in line outside the bathrooms. I'll never forget the nice little old man who I saw spraying cologne and brushing lint off of the guys' clothes. I thought to myself, "Wow, there are many opportunities to make money in America."

No Condition Is Permanent! *by Rene Godefroy*

The year was 1983. The afro was long gone, but I still had mine. I also still had my Haitian shoes and clothes... polyester bellbottoms! Many kids in Haiti kept up with fashion—I guess they could afford it. As for me, I was always a few years behind. I walked around in the club like a little lost soul, zigzagging my way through a maze of people. I felt and looked like a total stranger—and I was. Have you ever been to a social gathering and you didn't know what the dress code was? I was definitely not dressed for the occasion. I looked like an alien.

Finally, I saw a young lady who looked like she was looking for someone to dance with. I was so nervous! I went inside my mind trying to remember how to ask her in English. I went over to her, wiggled my hips a little bit and said one word, "Dance?" The woman stepped back and checked out my clothes and my Afro. She turned me down with an attitude that said, "You look weird!" I was so embarrassed. Have you ever felt rejected before? You know how I felt. I took it very personally. I wanted to find out what was wrong with me. I went to Philip and asked him why had the woman looked at me so condescendingly. "What's wrong with me?" I asked. He told me I needed a makeover; my Afro and clothes were kind of antique.

Have you ever had that happen to you? You are out with a friend and you have some stuff in your eyes or something is showing through your clothes, but they don't tell you. Somehow they figure you just want to make a fashion statement. Do you know what I am talking about? I was a bit upset at Philip. He could have saved me lots of trouble by telling me up front what I needed to do to look like the crowd. Friends help their friends. I guess Philip was afraid that he might have hurt my feelings.

Again, after my conversation with Philip, I decided to reinvent myself. If I were going to blend with the crowd at Big Daddy's, I needed a new look and attitude. I was determined to do something about my appearance and behavior. I realized the game had changed. The old thinking—my old mentality—was not going to help me party with the crowd.

I saw a guy at Big Daddy's who was the life of the party. He was like a social butterfly—the kind of guy who never meets a stranger. He was always on the dance floor dancing with different women. Have you ever met those kinds of people at parties? They kind of make you sick, don't they? I said to myself, "Hey, I'm not from here and I don't know what's going on, so I'd better find me a role model." Guest who was the model? You got that right. It was Mr. Social Butterfly. You know what? You don't always have to reinvent the wheel. It's often best to find someone who is succeeding at whatever you want to do and model his or her success. In my case, I wanted to be able to get a dance and hopefully a date. Though I was unable to communicate in English, I was determined to, at least, look like I belonged to the place. It was all a matter of attitude.

I stood into a corner and began to pay careful attention to how my model was behaving. I registered the way he walked, talked, and dressed. I had a pretty good picture of him in my head. Later on at home, I spent the whole week rehearsing in front of a mirror. I also came to the conclusion that I had to change my look. I decided to make a bold fashion statement. I wanted to wear something that would 'wow' the crowd—something that would keep them talking about me long after the night. So, I went to K-mart and picked out some clothes (yep, Blue Light Special!). I also decided to do something about my Afro. Can you guess what I did? Nope, I didn't cut it. I put in a Jerry Curl! I was really hip. I had little curls dangling right and left on my forehead. I felt like Michael Jackson—all I needed were some gloves!

There was a big problem with my curl: the weather was 99 degrees and it was very humid. As I sat waiting for the bus, grease and sweat began dripping around my neck. My hair was frying— you could almost hear it sizzling! It was a big price for me to pay just to try to fit with the Big Daddy's crowd, but whatever it took, I had to change. I will never forget the Haitian who was always watching me whenever I was around her in her living room. One day I asked her what was the matter. She told me that she was just making sure I didn't lean on her new couch with my Jerry Curl.

So, empowered with my Jerry Curl and my K-mart look, my self-confidence hit the roof. I couldn't wait for Philip and Big Daddy's to see me. I woke very early on Saturday to go over my moves. I felt pretty good about myself. I believe one of life's secrets to success is preparation. I was determined to succeed, so I prepared. Right before I walked into Big Daddy's, I grabbed my little Jerry Curl activator spray and showered my hair with it. I mean, my curls were really activated! My hair was dripping so much you could say it was raining. My collar was soaked. Well, I knew that once the air blew through my hair a little, the curls would be hard and shiny. Life in America!

The moment I stepped inside the club, I started imitating the gentleman I had seen the week before. I began to walk with a slow drag. I moved my hands just like the brother. I had some napkins in my hand patting the back and front of my head. Hey, I am not from America. I thought that was the way to get noticed. They played a song where everyone was chanting the ROOF IS ON FIRE! Some of you might be old enough to remember that song. When the DJ wanted to pump the crowd, he would crank that song very loud. He would also turn on some strobe lights, which were a great compliment to my Jerry Curl. You know what I mean? The energy in the room was very high. It was time for me to get a dance.

"Excuse me Madame, would you like to dance?" I asked a young lady checking me out. Without a blink, she agreed. On the way to the dance floor, I kept fixing and moving my curls to impress her. I was young and naïve, even stupid at times. I didn't know how to do the American moves. In Haiti, as I can remember, dancing didn't demand that I exert lots of energy. The woman's dancing was so hyper she started dancing from her chair! On the dance floor, the woman turned around and gave me her back. With both hands over her head she started bumping and pushing me with her behind. I said to myself, "Oh, my lord, I am in trouble!" I glanced around to see where the exit door was. Have you ever experienced the 'fight or flight' feeling? That was how I felt.

The dance floor was tiny with lots of people. The woman kept bumping me. I felt like a basketball bouncing back and forth between people. The crowd sang, pushed, and clapped, "The roof, the roof is on fire! We don't need no water! Let the…" Meanwhile, I was thinking to myself that my dance partner certainly needed some water. In fact, a whole fire truck would do for her. When the song finally ended, I let out a big sigh of relief. I felt liberated. It was a helluva experience for me. I began to think twice about whether I really wanted to join the Jerry Curl crowd. In the end, I was very glad I had. I had learned a lot about what a change in attitude can do for a person.

You Gotta Change With Change

Have you ever met people who think the world revolves around them? The moment they come into your territory, be it work, church, or home, they want you to change things their way. They could care less about how you feel as long as they get what they want. These people also often complain about the way things used to be. That is the way of rattlesnakes. Bees are so quick to learn new ways to do things; they look for the good.

One of the greatest lessons I learned from my experience at Big Daddy's is that you can change the world around you once you change your world. I am talking about an attitude shift. Being positively charged is the ability to embrace change and discover how we can benefit from it. My first thought at the club was one of fear and rebellion. I was facing the unknown in a way that created mixed emotions. I was happy to be in America, yet at the same time, I wasn't prepared to face the incredible changes I had to go through. Thank God my survival instincts from my village taught me to have what I call uncommon flexibility. It's an attitude that says: Be like a tree. When the wind is violent, flex with it.

I didn't expect the people at Bid Daddy's to get rid of their Jerry Curl and go back to Afro because of me, nor did I expect them to dance a different dance. People with a BEE attitude are sensitive to the needs of others. They spend time finding out how they can combine their strengths—the things they do right—with others in order to make things better. Yes, there was incredible pressure on me to adapt. That's beyond the point. There are many people who come to this country but who are so rigid that they rebel against change. You can see by observing them what little they have accomplished. They are like glass; they break into pieces in the face of change. I am not one of them. I decided to change. I believe you should live your life with an attitude of uncommon flexibility, too.

A Parting Comment

My friend, let me tell you this: You will never achieve anything without first going through the fire of change. Diamonds must sustain incredible amounts of heat and pressure before making their way to the homes of the rich and famous. You, too, have to go through the same process before you can find yourself on the mountaintop of success—no matter how you define success. It all happens when you walk around with a BEE attitude—a positively charged attitude.

Homework Assignment

Decide what changes you are willing to go through in order to get what you want. Remember this: Five years from now, you will be in the same job, making the same amount of money, living in the same house, and driving the same car if you are not willing to create change in your life today.

CHAPTER NINE

Create A
Positive Reputation

Create A
Positive Reputation

*"Whatever you lend, let it be your money, and not your name.
Money you may get again, and if not, you may contrive to do
without it; name once lost you cannot get again."*
—Edward Bulwer-Lytton

We were on a big American airline. Some passengers were going to visit, while others were returning home. The passengers included business dignitaries, students, and natives. Flying was nothing new to me, since I had flown to many different states before. However, that one trip was the most exhilarating one I have ever had. I was returning to my beloved village in Haiti for a visit, nine years after I had come to America to make my way into the world. Returning home after that length of time was an uplifting experience.

As I sat on the airplane, my fellow passengers and I discussed politics, economics and business. While my accent clearly indicated to them that America was not my native land, they were impressed with how much I knew about this country. They had no idea that a short few years earlier I had arrived in America a poor, shy, introverted young man with only basic education. They had no idea what I went through to reinvent myself. What a difference a few years of personal development can make! Have you ever evaluated yourself and found out that you had definitely changed? That is exactly how I felt seated on that airplane. I had changed; I had grown.

eft

As we neared the end of our flight, a voice came over the intercom: "Flight attendants prepare for arrival." The airplane turned around sharply over our destination, Port-au-Prince. I looked outside the window to get an overhead view of my country. What I saw was shocking! I saw a small section of the city where the rich folks reside. I had never seen this part of my country before. If someone had told me that such extravagant homes existed, I probably would have refuted it because I had never visited those ritzy neighborhoods. I am talking about homes that cost millions! Then the airplane flew over the large sections of Haiti where the masses are living broke, sick, and oppressed. That reminded me of the unfairness and injustice that I had experienced while living there. I had lived among those people; I understood their plight. I remembered how there was almost no opportunity to break the barrier of poverty. As I sat on the plane staring out the window, I wondered what my life would have been like if I hadn't ventured to America—if I hadn't stepped out of my tight shell. My heart overflowed with gratitude!

A Happy Return To The Village

Although we have no telephones, electricity, or broadcasting agencies in my village, news there travels very fast. Nevertheless, I was still amazed at how quickly my fellow villagers found out that I had returned for a visit. How had they known? They knew the same way that people in a company, church, family, or community know: one person had discovered that I was coming home, and soon everyone knew. Lots of folks turned out to greet me. People lined both sides of the road; they waved to me as I rode past. Many didn't even know me, but the sight of any automobile entering our village created excitement. Then I met a crowd of people who knew me well. They chased my ride all the way until we stopped. It felt like a holiday or a big parade with me as Grand Marshall.

Many who came to greet me did so hoping to get some money, while others came simply to see if I were indeed the boy they once had predicted wouldn't survive to adulthood. What about your village—work, church, and friends? Have you ever returned and generated that kind of excitement? Let me tell you, it's an amazing feeling.

Seeing my village again after all those years was eye opening. Although I had changed enormously, the folks who had remained in the village hadn't changed much. Most of them were still walking barefoot and half-naked. Their way of thinking was the same, too. They were confined to a tight mental shell. The village hadn't changed much, either. I could still find my way around. One thing that had changed was that the little house in which I had lived as a child was gone. The villagers told me the ocean took it away one night during a hurricane. Many of the people I knew had died.

As I moved about the village, the women customarily kissed me on my cheek and the men shook my hand. I could read the excitement on their faces as they greeted me. I shared lots of U.S. dollars with them. Their comments were poignant. Some said in Creole, "Li chappe," meaning "he made it". Others couldn't believe I was standing in front of *them*. That day, I heard an earful of how bad I had been as a kid. In addition, the folks in the village never cease to remind me how bad life was for me.

Then Alfred, an old villager, pushed through the crowd and began to speak. He said, "Now, all of you come here to remind him of his past because you expect some money. Why didn't you give him some encouragement when he needed it? After today, I hope you will learn to be kinder to the unfortunate kids in this village. This is a lesson for all of you to learn. Treat people with respect, regardless of their circumstances. Look at Rene; he never forgets us. He sends money to us all the time. Today, we must all agree that he is our village hero." Everyone repeated in unison, "You are right. Rene is our village hero!"

Alfred's words energized me. They touched me, too—I had to fight back the tears. It was nice for him to say those kind words about me, but in reality, I didn't consider myself a hero then, and I still don't now. I do believe that I am a testimony to the world that *No Condition Is Permanent!,* that there is more to what meets the eye in every one of us. God is awesome all the time! If I am indeed a village hero, everyone has the potential of becoming one. Wolfgang von Goethe wrote, "Treat a man as he is and he will remain as he is. Treat a man as he can and should be, and he will become as he can and should be." When was the last time you looked at someone and imagined what he or she could be? Better yet, has someone treated you that way lately? What kind of reputation do you have? Are you a bee or a rattlesnake?

Your Reputation Is Your Treasure

To experience the kind of feeling in your village that I felt in mine, you have to develop an excellent reputation. We didn't and still don't have a credit system back home. We have no credit cards or credit bureaus. The only thing one can depend on for credit is one's reputation. Your reputation is the most precious thing you can own. The man without a great reputation is also a very unfortunate man. What do people say about you when you are not around and your name comes up? Can others count on you? Do you keep your word? It is said that the oil billionaire J. Paul Getty had such a great reputation that his handshake was enough to seal a deal.

Your reputation is also your personal brand. You should invest a lot of energy into building your brand. How do you do that? Don't forget about the people at the bottom. Always find ways to encourage and uplift them. Remember what I said before. You can always tell a big person—a village hero—by the way he or she treats little people. When you make a promise, keep your word to others. If you can't do something, just say so. Assume that you are always on stage; always do the right thing.

You Can Make A Difference

My return trip to Haiti became one of soul searching and contemplation. As I went past village after village observing the needy kids, I asked myself, "Will they ever be aware of what they are capable of achieving?" I looked at the beggars living in the gutters by the side of the road. I asked myself, "Do they know how many gifts and talents are buried inside of them?" I realized that those people were once precious babies being rocked in their mother's arms. I am certain that their mothers, either consciously or subconsciously, had high aspirations for them.

What happened along the way? Could it be that the waves of life pushed them here and there, hopelessly on its shores? Then I asked myself, why aren't the heroes in their villages helping them to realize their inherent power? Why aren't their heroes helping them to foster positive self-esteem? Maybe there are no such heroes among them. Maybe I just don't have the answers to those questions.

If you and I are going to strive to become and stay village heroes, there are many things that will be expected of us. We must look for ways to contribute—to make a difference. Have you ever taken a moment to reflect upon your existence on this planet? Have you ever doubted that you mattered at all? Yes, your presence on this earth matters. Life is like a puzzle, and you are definitely one piece of the puzzle. When we realize the impact we can make through our everyday interactions with people, we begin to live on purpose. Whether you are rich or poor, attractive or unattractive, or a hundred other things, you are endowed with the awesome power and potential to positively change the lives of those with whom you come in contact.

I know that you and I will never be able to touch everybody. I can't identify with everybody. You can reach those that I can't and vice versa. That means that if you think you can't make a difference, you are making a huge mistake. You don't have to be a motivational speaker on stage speaking to thousands of people. You can tutor a child and help him discover his gifts. Do you see what I mean? You do a little, and I do a little, and together our efforts will amount to great things! It doesn't matter where we are. Not everyone in the village will rise to the task of becoming a village hero, but someone has to do it. That someone had better be you *and* me!

Connect And Impact From The Heart

Making a decision to become a village hero and to create a positive reputation starts at the center of the heart. The head does not know the way of the soul; that is the heart's function. Real connection happens in our heart. When I took that trip to my village, it was a journey to my heart. My purpose became clear to me. The head doesn't know anything about purpose, meaning, and significance. As a matter of fact, it often confuses and contradicts us. There is only one place where you can feel and know; it's your heart. Your heart makes you cry—and laugh. If you are familiar with the Bible, you may know King Solomon's words: a cheerful heart is good medicine.

As a village hero, you are called to connect with and impact others every time the opportunity arises. Many people call this chemistry; I call it heart. That is why I encourage you to get in touch with your heart more often. Isn't it ironic that we can travel far distances—literally to the moon and back, yet find it difficult to travel the short distance to our heart? That's where meaning and significance reside. Your heart will also tell you when you're dancing to the drumbeat of your life's music. Listen to your heart; it knows. Connect, connect, connect.

5 Characteristics Of A Village Hero

1) *The Village Hero Makes Peace And Forgives Others*
As a child growing up in the village, I never saw my father. He wasn't from my village, and he never came around while I was there. I did see him on three occasions in the City. To this day, if I saw my father, I wouldn't recognize him. I was too young when I saw him last. I grew up resenting him for his lack of responsibility as a parent, particularly when I found out that he had lots of other children in other villages. When we go through life hating or resenting others, we are actually carrying a monkey on our back. Since our life usually creates a domino effect, the monkey literally affects every part of our lives.

As I gained more insight and wisdom throughout my life, I felt the need to completely forgive my father. I wish I could meet him today, but I don't believe that's possible. Folks say he is dead. You see, my father is simply a product of society. His computer (his brain) was running the wrong software. He grew up registering faulty information that caused him to behave immorally. Tony McGee, a friend of mine, is right when he says that you can't blame someone who never had a teacher. As a village hero, you can't help the village if you resent its people.

That Little Thing We Call Guilt

When I arrived at the Haiti Airport, I was instructed not to share money with the poor kids hanging outside. It seems they too often fight each other for the money. I ignored the warning and shared a few dollars with the kids because I couldn't ignore their cry. Their voices tugged my heart. I knew their plight because I had been there. One kid tenaciously ran with the car as we were pulling away, yelling, "Sir, you forgot me!" I asked the driver to slow down so that I could give the poor guy some money; but he refused, and we sped off. For a long time I felt a sense of guilt about that. I had missed an opportunity to truly make a difference in someone's life. Guilt, guilt, guilt.

I know we have discussed this previously, but it bears revisiting here. Are you burdened down with guilt? Did something happen that you feel was your fault? No matter how bad you feel though, you cannot change the past. You may have wronged someone who will not forgive you. That's fine—you can't control others; but you must be willing to forgive yourself. Let your guilt go. Affirm to yourself that you are sorry, and forgive yourself for whatever it was that you have done. Then say (out loud, if you have to), "Now I am free of that burden!"

How To Get Rid Of The Monkey On Your Back

a) To release resentment, go to the place where you are holding the anger—go to your heart. Then say, in the form of prayer or meditation, "I am slowly releasing this person from my heart." You can go to the person and let him or her know you have done this, but that isn't necessary. Both of you may be carrying a burden, but your focus should be on releasing yours.

b) Take a paper and pen to a park or quiet place one evening and write down everything that you want to let go of on a separate piece of paper. Then crumble up the pieces and burn them while watching the flame and smoke rise. As the papers burn, imagine that a big load is being lifted from your shoulders. Smile. This exercise always works for me. It will for you, too.

c) Resolve to never say anything negative about the person or talk about the situation with others. When someone else mentions the person's name in a condescending manner, say something nice, change the subject, or walk away. Again, I know I have said this to you before but it is so powerful, I can never say it enough.

The beauty of doing these things is that it puts you in the driver's seat. The day you can truly forgive and let go is the day you will start your journey to becoming a village hero. If you haven't already, why don't you start that journey now!

2) The Village Hero Is A Contributor
In our personal and professional lives, we learn how to succeed from those who come before us. They are the pathmakers. We are the pathfinders. There comes a time when we have to change roles. We move from being pathfinders to pathmakers, from being mentees to mentors. Have you made a difference in someone's life recently? What footprints are you leaving behind? Do you give as you take? My greatest joy in life is having a sense of contribution. Whether I am giving money or advice to a person, I am making a difference in that person's life and mine, too.

I want to stress that you don't have to give money to be a pathmaker. Your time, advice, and praise are just as good. Perhaps you are already making a difference through your work. If your customers' lives are better because of what you provide, then you are making a major difference in the world. Congratulations! You should not take it for granted. Once you embrace an attitude of service, you will wake up every day with more passion and a stronger commitment. What's more, you will become a village hero to your customers.

3) A Village Hero Uses Stories To Inspire Others

Many beginning speakers say they don't have a story to tell about their life. They believe that because they haven't climbed Mount Everest, didn't grow up in a tiny village in Haiti, or weren't at one time a prisoner of war, they don't have a life story interesting enough or unique enough to inspire others. Far from it! If you are living, your life is full of stories that can inspire the uninspired. Unfortunately, many of you are waiting for things to get perfect before you start. In the meantime, those who are supposed to be blessed by you are suffering from your procrastination. Village heroes learn how to impact and inspire others through stories.

Members of my audiences rarely remember my name. Of course, it's hard to remember Godefroy, but they all know me by my stories. They say, "Do you remember this guy who spoke to our group five years ago? I am talking about the guy who came to America from underneath a tractor-trailer." My stories have become my brand. Stories connect us. People don't remember facts, figures, and ideas as much as they remember stories. I discovered the power of storytelling through my observation of other speakers. To leverage that information, I took a class on storytelling and began to listen to storytellers.

Your personal stories are therapeutic to others. They help others jump their hurdles. Your stories also help you connect with others. You would not believe how many people have shared their stories with me after I have shared mine. When you share a personal story with others, you are basically telling them they are safe to open up and share with you. People usually don't reveal who they are with us until we first share a part of ourselves with them. Whatever you and I went through at some point in our life, someone is going through a similar situation now. When we share our story with the person, we are telling him or her that *No Condition is Permanent!*

Exercise

Think for a few moments, then jot down a "story" from your life that you feel will inspire and encourage others. What did you learn from it that others can use?

4) Village Heroes Don't Blame Others And They Don't Make Excuses

All of us have a tendency to blame others for our circumstances. If you told me that you never blame anyone else, I would strongly doubt it. Blaming is the first impulse we have when something negative happens. (You'll notice I said something negative. When something positive happens, people fight to take the credit.) What's more, some people are consumed with blame. At the blink of an eye, they can tell you exactly who or what is to blame for their situation. When there is no one else to blame, they often blame God!

Blaming others is a game we learn to play at an early age. As children, we often say, "It wasn't me. Mary did it," or "Peter did it." As adults, we continue to blame others in our personal and professional lives. We don't meet the company's goals because one department lacks initiative. The husband blames the wife for his lack of patience or affection. At work, the first shift blames the second shift for their failure to make production. It becomes a vicious cycle of shifting blame. Finger pointing never solves a problem; it only escalates tension. When taken to the extreme, we find nations blaming each other until a full-fledged war breaks out.

I cringe when I see people on national television blaming something that happened to them twenty years ago when they were children for what they do or don't do today. I'm not discounting the fact that a past trauma can create an emotional block-age later in life, but you can release the trauma. You don't believe me? Well, there have been many documented cases of people who grew up in the same or similar dysfunctional environments with abusive and/or alcoholic parents. Some of those abused become highly successful; others become total failures. The difference is that those who fail spend all their energy blaming their parents or their past. They are often known as whiners. Mother Teresa said it best when she said, "Yesterday is gone. Tomorrow has not yet come. We have only today. Let us begin." Village heroes know that their future depends on the choices they make today.

I met a gentleman, Mike, in Athens, Georgia. He attended the University of Georgia for more than four years, and graduated with a degree in English. He has a passion for writing advertising copy. Can you guess what Mike is doing now for a living? Your answer will probably be, writing. I'm sorry to disappoint you; Mike has been a prep cook at a restaurant for seven years, making $8 an hour, and he hates it. When I asked Mike why he wasn't doing what he loves, he gave me a thousand excuses. In other words, he blamed things and circumstances for the losing life he was living.

I told Mike my story, and we bonded. I made him aware of his excuses. Then I gave him several great ideas to help him leverage his writing skills. Mike was beside himself with joy. He had no idea there were so many things he could begin immediately to start living his dream of becoming a writer. Mike later asked me where I learned about marketing. I told him I learned the ideas I had shared with him from books, and those same books are waiting for him at the bookstores and libraries. I felt like a charismatic preach-er. I snatched away all Mike's mental crutches, and encouraged him to take full responsibility for his life.

What are your excuses? What is holding you back from living your dreams? Are you waiting until all the lights in your life are green to start the journey? I am sorry to say that this will never happen. Be a village hero. Yesterday is gone. Tomorrow hasn't come. Live your life today!

5) *Village Heroes Have Strong Principles*

One day I was working at the hotel when one of the bellmen, Ali, came from the inside with a cart piled high with luggage. He handed the cart to me at the door and told me to load the luggage into Dr. Barbara King's car. Dr. King is a very good tipper, so good that we usually allow her chauffeur to park in a VIP space near the front of the hotel. Five minutes later, her chauffeur walked by and tipped me. The bellman then came out and insisted that the tip belonged to him. I told him that this is what Dr. King customarily tips me. He told me that Dr. King herself would tip me later and that this tip was his, so I gave him the money.

Sure enough, I later received a tip from Dr. King. I politely said thank you and pocketed the money. Before they took off, Dr. King called me over and asked, "My chauffeur said she had already given you a tip. Why did you take mine?" I could hear disappointment in her tone of voice. Embarrassed, I began explaining what had happened, but I could see that it was hard for her to buy my story. They drove off and I stood there devastated!

Later, Ali told me that he had been playing a practical joke on me, and that he hadn't done any work for Dr. King. He hadn't actually brought the cart. He met the chauffeur by the door and opened it for her. I had worked with the guy for years and know that he is a decent and honest gentleman. To this day, I respect him highly. I know my friend was kidding, but his timing was not good at all. In the end, I had to live with the embarrassment.

I'm sure Dr. Barbara King has forgotten about the incident. As one of America's most prominent preachers, her philosophy is based on forgiveness; but I couldn't forget what had happened. My integrity and character had been on the line, and I had failed. I explained the situation to my co-worker, Robert Hampton. Robert is my play dad, someone I respect immensely. He assured me that he would talk to Dr. King for me the next time she returned; but from then on, every time I noticed her car, I hid because I didn't know how to face her.

I believe I obtained my strong principles from my maman. Maman was very poor, but she made sure that my brother, sister, and I had honesty and decency as the cornerstones of our lives. I vividly remember the day I took a dime from her pocketbook without first asking her permission. When Maman asked me about the missing dime, I lied to her; but I got caught. I was very hungry, so I took the dime and bought a piece of cassava (a kind of cracker made out a vegetable named manioc (mahn yok)) from Mrs. Robert, a neighbor in the City. Mrs. Robert suspected something was wrong because I walked away without asking for my change. At the time, I didn't know what a dime was. I thought it was the equivalent of a penny. Mrs. Robert told Maman what I had done. Boy, did I get a mean whooping—one I will never forget. Maman beat me with a cowhide whip as if she didn't know me. Wham, wham! "You are not going to disgrace and embarrass me," she yelled. Wham, wham! "I am not raising a thief in the family. Never lie to me again!"

Maman was right. From that day on, I never did anything that might disgrace her. There comes a time when you have to stand by your principles, when you must refuse to compromise. When temptation comes, village heroes ask themselves, "Is this the right thing to do? Can I live with this decision in peace for the rest of my life?"

We may appear to escape getting caught doing unethical things, but we can't escape from ourselves. Somehow, whatever we do always comes back to haunt us. There are those who don't care. They are numb and apathetic. That is why we have so many troubles in the world today. You are not one of those people. You are a village hero. You know even when there is no one watching, your reputation is at stake. You want others to mention your name in a positive way. You keep your word. You safeguard your reputation.

uaa suvauecvvaavanikk aaa aaafjcafjj auuuu uuuuu uuuueuauurrrvvev

Now that you know how to become a village hero, it's time to Alfretize your life. Go out and spot village heroes and let them know it. Alfred did it for me, I'm doing it for others, and I'm counting on you to do the same. Commit incredible acts and you will intensify your personal brand.

CHAPTER TEN

Practice Unbounded Gratitude

Practice Unbounded Gratitude

"If one should give me a dish of sand, and tell me there were particles of iron in it, I might look for them with my eyes, and search for them with my clumsy fingers, and be unable to detect them; but let me take a magnet and sweep through it and how would it draw to itself the almost invisible particles by the mere power of attraction. The unthankful heart, like my finger in the sand, discovers no mercies; but let the thankful heart sweep though the day, and as the magnet finds the iron, so it will find, in every hour, some heavenly blessing. Only the iron in God's sand is gold!" —Henry Ward Beecher

When I returned to my village, I had lots of stories to share with my fellow villagers. I told them stories of markets filled with food flown in from around the world; stories of doctors who gave out pills to stop people from eating; stories of lives so empty of physical labor that people ran around in circles so their hearts wouldn't die. I told the villagers stories of roads flatter than a midnight sea; stories of cars so numerous they clogged the roads and slowed the traffic to the pace of a bicycle. I also told them of Armageddon prophets predicting the fall of humanity over a computer calendar glitch—Y2K.

My fellow villagers couldn't believe Americans faced these problems. Why? The villagers considered these things blessings! I went on to tell them that the problems created something Americans called *stress*. I could see the quizzical looks on their

faces. They had never heard the word 'stress' until I mentioned it
to them, just as I had never heard it until I came here. "Why do
they let such petty things bother them so much?" one woman
asked me. I told her that I didn't know.

I don't want to pretend that Americans don't have their own
share of problems. Now, more than ever, we have a lot to worry
about. Our freedoms are being compromised. What I am referring
to are those little inconveniences that we label 'problems'. My
goal is to help you keep things in perspective and to encourage you
to focus on what is important. Focus on your priorities. I also want
to encourage you to shift your attitude from one of being discon-
tent to one of being grateful for what you have.

Count Your Blessings

Let's say you give your child everything he or she wants. You
work hard doing two jobs because you want your child to have the
very best. You even neglect yourself in the process. One day your
child comes to you complaining. He or she tells you that you
aren't doing enough because other kids wear $100 tennis shoes
and you only buy $50 shoes for him or her. Wouldn't your child's
complaints stab you in the heart? Would this encourage you to
give even more to the child?

What if things were the other way around? What if your child
is always kissing you and hugging you to thank you for all the
things you provide. He or she tells everybody about your sacrifices. You would feel so good about your child that you would
want to give him or her the world. Do you see how either a grateful or an ungrateful heart can either open the floodgates of abundance or slam them shut?

Don't you think the way you would feel about the ungrateful
child is how your Creator feels about you sometimes? Do you go
to church praying for a five-bedroom house instead of one with
three bedrooms? What if you give thanks for the one you have
instead? There are thousands of things that we can be grateful for
every single day. Instead, though, we complain to God. Perhaps

you and I should focus on giving thanks to God instead of praying to Him for more. Wow, what a concept! A grateful heart is the way to receive more. Have you ever noticed how much more people are willing to do for you when you praise and thank them? That is the key to an abundant life.

Let's take something as simple as food. Did you know that the average American throws away about $1,000 worth of food in the trash every year? Did you also know that in many parts of the world there are millions of people starving to death? Those starving people thank God when the relief truck brings them food. How is that for a different attitude?

How To Instantly Go From Sadness To Happiness

Many of us suffer from a terrible disease that sends us into depressive moods more often than we can imagine. I call this disease gratitude deficiency. Once we become complacent and begin to take for granted what we have, gratitude deficiency sneaks up on us. My friend, Jan Toles, once was having a tough day. I asked her to tell me her problems. In less than five minutes, I was able to assist her in reframing her thinking. I reminded her how God continues to pour his blessings into her each and every day. I challenged Jan to get into a 'gratitude mode.' She said with a chuckle, "Thank you for helping me keep things in perspective." She sounded upbeat and ready to take on the day.

Would you like to know how to instantly go from being unhappy to being happy? *Just shift your focus from what you're lacking to all that you should be grateful for.* It's impossible to be unhappy or stressed and to be grateful at the same time. How could that be? Think about it; the mind can only hold one thought at a time, though it may process these thoughts at the speed of light. The key is to flood your mind with thoughts of gratitude throughout the day. One way to do this is to focus on your successes instead of your failures, or on your strengths instead of your weaknesses. Each time you succeed, you gain more self-confidence. Why not enlarge those successful moments in your mind on a daily basis?

Make a *gratitude list* then review it frequently. This list will help you remember all that you have to be thankful for.

Don't Let The Traffic Get To You

How many of you have been stuck in traffic? If you live in or around a major city, that happens to you pretty much every day. What do you do when there are cars all around you and you're barely moving? Have you ever yelled at other drivers? Have you honked your horn? Have you thrown up your hands in frustration? Get a grip! We are talking about traffic, not death or sickness. Keep your blood pressure down. When you find yourself frustrated in traffic, you are being ungrateful. A crowded highway is the price we pay for being an abundant and successful nation. No Condition is Permanent!; the more we have, the more things change. We must be willing to lose something in order to enjoy something else.

When I'm stuck in traffic, I remember Voici Phane. For the first several years of my life in Haiti, Voici Phane was the only vehicle of any kind that I knew. It was a battered old truck, ancient and loud, that brought people to and from the village once every week. For many years, I waited for that truck every single week. I looked at all the women getting off, hoping that one of them would be my Maman. I asked them, "Have you seen my mother? Did she find a job? Did she send for me?" None of them knew Maman's whereabouts. Every week, I waited for Voici Phane, certain that one day it would bring Maman to me. It was my only hope and it was the only automobile I expected to see for the day.

Do you see where I am going with this? How frustrated are you when you see lots of cars blocking the lanes? As a little boy, anxiously waiting to meet Maman, I would have loved to see dozens of trucks, or even a crowded highway. I would have been filled with more hope because surely one of those many trucks would have brought Maman to me. Don't you understand? It's not the event that frustrates us; it's what we say to ourselves about the event. Now, when I find myself stuck in traffic, not only do I remember Voici Phane, but I also give thanks for the fortune that has allowed me to own and drive my very own car on smooth roads. In other words, I count my blessings. I also use this opportunity to educate myself. I always have personal development tapes to listen to in my car. I turn my driving time into learning time.

Choices, Choices, Choices

While many people around the world go to bed every night hungry, we debate over where and what we are going to eat. For many people here and in other well-developed countries, dinner can cost as much as $300. I don't mean to make you feel guilty. Au contraire, I am encouraging you to take pleasure and enjoy the abundance the good Lord provides for you. Have you ever heard people say things like, "I am so unhappy that I can't even enjoy a meal?" What they are really saying is, "I don't have a grateful heart." Man, when I have a plate of rice and chicken in front of me, I am so thankful.

Tom Bell, an excellent writer, told me of this experience. Once, while he was eating in an expensive restaurant, he watched a woman send a Porterhouse steak back to the chef because it had been cooked medium instead of medium-rare. Later, he watched a man who was dining with the woman struggle to decide whether to have orange sherbet for dessert and stick to his diet, or splurge on an ice cream sundae dripping with caramel and piled with pecans. Does any of this sound familiar? I don't want to sound unsympathetic. I know how important and difficult a diet can be. I know we all want our food to taste good, especially when we're paying a lot of money. But when Tom told me that story, I thought of a mountain of breadfruit.

Remember the breadfruit I described earlier? I doubt you would ever be able to find them in your nearby grocery store. Outside, they look similar to a pineapple; but inside, they taste like a tough, extra-starchy potato. As a child, I ate almost nothing but breadfruit. The folks in my village cook it creatively. They boil it and fry it.

They even beat it to a pulp and dip it in okra sauce. I ate breadfruit every day. My tongue grew so accustomed to it that I ceased to taste it at all. I only ate it for survival. My bloated stomach struggled to digest all the starch. So now when I must choose between ice cream and sherbet, I give thanks to God for the great fortune I've had. It's a blessing to be able to choose what's for dinner.

As I mentioned earlier, no one in my village understood the concept of stress. How could they? Eating only breadfruit, traveling on their bare feet, relying on the moon for light at night, they didn't know what stress was. They only knew that I lived in a land of great abundance. (They knew that I drove my own car, that I ate lunch in restaurants with six-page menus, and that I could light a room, path or road with an electric light whenever I chose.) Am I saying that my fellow villagers don't get upset? Of course they do; but they don't call it stress. Besides, when you compare the little things that stress you versus what they go through, they are the ones who should be stressed. Yes, sometimes you can have real problems, but I am not talking about those.

Y2K After Midnight

Remember the Y2K bug? How could you not? Every "expert" who had ever turned on a computer was predicting that civilization would screech to a horrible halt after midnight, December 31, 1999. They predicted that all the microchips wouldn't know what day it was. The lights would go out, the elevators would stop, and our bank accounts would be wiped-out. I didn't worry, though, as midnight approached on that so-called dooms day. A lady tried to scare me by telling me that it was going to be the end of the world, but I was unfazed. Instead, I told the lady that it was going to be the end of her world.

December 1999 was a matter of perspective. I saw it differently than many others. I hoped that everything would be okay. In fact, secretly, I kind of wanted the lights to go out. We had no electricity in my village in Haiti. The only streetlights I ever saw were the headlights of the Voici Phane. When nightfall came, we had to walk very carefully outside our homes. There were no streetlights to show us the thorns before we stepped on them, no flashlights to show us the stones before we tripped on them. Only on nights with a dazzling full moon could we find our way around with ease. Think about it; I was born Y2K ready!

In America, I rarely see the stars. The streetlights are too bright, as are the billboards and the headlights. The storefront display lights and the used-car-sale spotlights. And so on and so on. The artificial lights outshine the stars and compete with the moon. I could certainly enjoy a night or two without all that interference blocking Mother Nature. I could once again dance with my shadow under a full moon. Thank God Y2K didn't happen because too many wouldn't know how to handle it. I would have been one of the very few who would have been calm. I would also have been one of the very few to remember that *No Condition is Permanent!*, and that we still have thousands of things to be grateful for.

Size 9 Sir, Don't Forget!

His name is Petion. He is fifteen years old. He came to my village from another faraway village hoping to find a better life. I met Petion during my last trip back to Haiti. We went for a walk and climbed the hills together as he gave me a tour of the land surrounding my village. He showed me where he came from. I asked Petion about his brothers and sisters. He told me he doesn't know them because his mother gave them away to strangers, hoping they would be better off. I told Petion about my story—about how I started and how bad I had it. He couldn't believe it! "Sir, you look so different now," he said. "Petion," I told him, "that's right, but in my heart I never forget where I started."

After about thirty minutes of walking and climbing, I got tired and was perspiring. We sat down to take a break. Petion became very quiet. He took a good look at me from head to toe. He then looked at himself. He was barefoot, and he wore ragged, tarnished clothes. I asked him, "What's the matter? You are looking at me and you are not talking." He said to me, "Sir, do you have lots of shoes?" I said, "Yes, why do you ask?" Petion told me, "I pray for the day when I would get my first pair of shoes. I never had any before, Sir. That's my dream." He paused; then he continued, "Oh, I would shine them every day."

You know what? Being with Petion reminded me that I need to be grateful. Until then, it had never occurred to me that I had lots of shoes in my closet. "Petion, your dream will come true one day," I said. "I will send you some shoes." He smiled and said, "Thank you, Sir. I tried someone's shoes before. They fit well and they are size nine. You can send me size nine, Sir." It was time for me to leave. "Petion, I have to go. Don't worry, you will get some shoes." I stood and he remained seated with a sad look on his face. Right before I walked away, Petion flashed nine of his fingers at me and said, "Size nine, don't forget. I am counting on you!"

How many pair of shoes do you own? How many don't you wear anymore? Do you still have some brand new shoes that you may have forgotten about? You should put shoes on your gratitude list. I'm trying to help you see that you are blessed beyond measure! Do you know how many people around the world would gladly trade places with you in spite of all your problems? Regardless of what "problems" we may be facing, we are still a thousand times better off than most other people. It's one thing to have problems; it's another to be starting with a truckload of problems.

Right now, there are many people around the world picking and preparing what you will buy at your grocery store tomorrow. Those people are laboring for pennies to prepare your groceries. What about the clothes, jewelry, and shoes you wear? Do you know the very same laborers who make those items usually can't afford the luxury of wearing or eating their own products? My friend, it's time for a gratitude check. Every now and then, I go through the routine of asking myself what else I should be grateful for. It's usually a refreshing and relaxing experience. Try it and judge for yourself .

It's All A Matter Of Perspective

The year 2001 was a tough year for most speakers, trainers, and consultants. The economy was slowing down significantly. Companies were letting thousands of people go. Then the attack on the World Trade Center in New York sent our nation into a whirlwind. Unexpectedly, a full-fledge war broke out on terrorism, with much uncertainty about the outcome.

Many speakers say they didn't do well at all that year. You know what? It was my best year ever. I made a lot of money speaking. You may say, "I bet he made a million dollars." Well, I didn't say I made more money than the other speakers. In fact, some of those same speakers made fifty times more than I did. They consider that to be a bad year. I had never made much money in life. What I made that year was just enough for me to get by. However, it was more than I had made the previous year. I was so grateful. I considered myself fortunate because I still made more than lots of people in this country and around the world. It's not the event; it's our interpretation of the event.

The Land Of Plenty

When I entered the United States my only possession was a battered, little suitcase with two shirts and a single pair of pants. I had $5 in my pocket. Today, I have more than I could ever imagine. I am an American citizen living the American Dream. Looking back at my start in life in a tiny Haitian village, I am one of the most grateful people living in this country. You will never really know how good you have it until you visit poor countries to see what some people go through.

Do you remember a time when you were so anxious because a significant event was about take place in your life? Perhaps it was the day of your wedding, a big promotion, a graduation, or the birth of a newborn baby. Whatever it was, you just couldn't wait for it to happen. For me, that day was the day I was going to be inducted as a citizen of this nation. I was about to pledge allegiance to the United States of America—the land about which I am so grateful. What a privilege!

As I raised my right hand, my mind was flooded with pictures of my childhood. As a child, my biggest dream was to come here to make something of myself. When they handed me my citizenship documents, I felt like I was given a passport to achieve all that I had hoped for. I am sure there are a few ungrateful immigrants to this land who may feel annoyed by my comments about the U.S. I don't mean to step on anybody's toes but since I am talking about gratitude, I might as well express mine. I came here because I was looking for opportunities to improve my life, and I found them. If it were better in my country, I would never have left my family, friends, and my culture behind in order to settle in a strange land with a strange language and culture. If I didn't like it here, I would be living somewhere else. Life is just too short.

Freedom Is Sweet

If you asked me what I enjoy most in the U.S., I will say my freedom. What about you? Do you really understand how precious freedom is? It's easy to take something for granted when we've had it all our lives. As for me, I remember growing up without my freedom. I remember watching the injustice and brutality of the dictatorship led by Papa Doc, and, later, his son, Baby Doc. I remember not having the freedom to express my thoughts in public or around my own family because I was so afraid of the tonton macoutes—the government watchdogs.

I salute from the bottom of my heart the men and women who consecrated their lives to build this strong and powerful nation. I particularly take my hat off to the founding fathers of this nation for their vision. They started from scratch and led this country to economic prosperity. I am not saying things are perfect here, but this is a great country. That is why some people risk their lives to come here.

Freedom is what makes a nation bloom and prosper. It is not knowledge or information alone that makes a nation great; it is the freedom to use and apply the knowledge creatively. All right, I have conveyed my gratitude to you. Now, it is time to convey your own gratitude in your own way. Don't be cheap when it comes to giving thanks, or you will block the flow of abundance in your life.

It's Been Real

Yes, yes, I have truly enjoyed spending time with you; but, now, may I ask you a favor? No, I don't need your money; and no, I'm not asking you for a donation to the Village Hero Foundation. I'm asking you for something that is far more significant than anything else you will ever do. Think about the ideas you learned from me, or any others that came to mind while you were reading. Would you make it a point to share your new ideas and perspectives with as many people as you can? I ask you to share because it is what grateful people do.

Epilogue

⚭

"Action may not always bring happiness; but there is no happiness without action."—Benjamin Disraeli

I congratulate you for taking time to read through this book, and all the more because you read it to the end. Statistics tell us that only a handful of people read books from cover to cover. You are obviously one of the elite few. However, you can read all the books on personal growth, listen to all the tapes, and spend time with the most successful people alive, yet still find yourself stuck in neutral. Simply put, I can bottle up all the ideas and strategies ever imagined and give them to you; but if all you do is think about them, guess what, nothing will ever happen!

Now is the time to take action—do something. Quit thinking about it. Maybe you are waiting for things to get right before you start. I've got news for you: things are never going to get right, at least not as right as you expect them to be. The rule of thumb when it comes to living your dreams is just start. Like they say, "If you want to have, you've got to do first."

The great philosopher Francis Bacon said, "Knowledge is power." Yeah, there is some truth to that statement. Yet I have also heard other people say that knowledge is only potential power. It is the application of knowledge that is power. I wholeheartedly agree. Have you ever met people who know so much yet they never put what they know into action? Listen, don't be one of

161

those people. Take action! If all you do is join an association, enroll in a computer class, or ask someone to mentor you do that much at least. Take your first step. Hurry up, I will be waiting at the top for you!

My Favorite Books

"If a man has come to that point where he is so content that he says, 'I do not want to know any more, or do any more, or be any more,' he is in a state in which he ought to be changed into a mummy."—Henry Ward Beecher

The Greatest Miracle by **Og Mandino**

Think And Grow Rich by **Napoleon Hill**

How to Win Friends and Influence People by **Dale Carnegie**

The Power of Positive Thinking by **Norman Vincent Peale**

As A Man Thinketh by **James Allen**

Thinking Big by **David J. Schwartz**

The Magic of Believing by **Claude M. Bristol**

How to Stop Worrying and Start Living by **Dale Carnegie**

7 Habits of Highly Effective People by **Stephen Covey**

Tough Times Never Last, but Tough People Do! by **Robert H. Schuller**

The Greatest Salesman In The World by **Og Manding**

Personal Power by **Anthony Robbins**

Seeds of Greatness by **Dr. Dennis Waitley**

Maximum Achievement by **Brian Tracy**

Rene Godefroy

Give The Gift Of No Condition Is Permanent!
To Someone You Care About

Order Form

No Condition Is Permanent!

Item	Unit Cost	Quantity	Total
Book	$20.00	_____	_____
T-shirt (XL only)	$14.00	_____	_____
Coffee Mug	$9.95	_____	_____
Poster	$9.95	_____	_____

Shipping & Handling

If Sub Total is:	USA	Canada
$0 - 25	$5	$10
$25 - 100	$9	$20
$100 - $200	$15	$30
$200 - 300	$25	$40
call for price on orders over $300		

ALL PRICES US DOLLARS

Canadian Shipping prices do not include duty, taxes or custom charges that could be charged at the border.

Sub Total:_____   **S & H:**_____   **Total:**_____

Name _____Date _____

Company _____

Street Address _____

City/Province _____

Zip Code _____Country _____Phone _____

Payment: ❑Amex   ❑Visa   ❑Master Card   ❑Check/Money Order

Credit Card Number: _____

Exp Date: _____Signature: _____

Village Hero, Inc. • P.O. Box 725169 • Atlanta, GA 31139
For Faster Service Call Toll Free:1-866-ASK-Rene (275-7363)
For local calls please call: (770) 438-1373
Internet: wwwReneSpeaks.com
Quantity discounts available on all products